Reimagine Pricing

Jan Y. Yang
Reimagine Pricing

How AI is Changing Everything

Jan Y. Yang
Simon-Kucher and Partners
Frankfurt am Main, Germany

ISBN 978-3-031-90417-2   ISBN 978-3-031-90418-9 (eBook)
https://doi.org/10.1007/978-3-031-90418-9

© The Editor(s) (if applicable) and The Author(s), under exclusive license to Springer Nature Switzerland AG 2025

This work is subject to copyright. All rights are solely and exclusively licensed by the Publisher, whether the whole or part of the material is concerned, specifically the rights of reprinting, reuse of illustrations, recitation, broadcasting, reproduction on microfilms or in any other physical way, and transmission or information storage and retrieval, electronic adaptation, computer software, or by similar or dissimilar methodology now known or hereafter developed.

The use of general descriptive names, registered names, trademarks, service marks, etc. in this publication does not imply, even in the absence of a specific statement, that such names are exempt from the relevant protective laws and regulations and therefore free for general use.

The publisher, the authors and the editors are safe to assume that the advice and information in this book are believed to be true and accurate at the date of publication. Neither the publisher nor the authors or the editors give a warranty, expressed or implied, with respect to the material contained herein or for any errors or omissions that may have been made. The publisher remains neutral with regard to jurisdictional claims in published maps and institutional affiliations.

This Springer imprint is published by the registered company Springer Nature Switzerland AG.
The registered company address is: Gewerbestrasse 11, 6330 Cham, Switzerland

If disposing of this product, please recycle the paper.

I extend my heartfelt gratitude to my editor, Jialin Yan, and her dedicated colleagues at Springer for their invaluable support. While the pleasure of creating this work is entirely mine, so too are any errors that remain.

Competing Interests

The author has no competing interests to declare that are relevant to the content of this manuscript.

About this Book

AI-Enabled Pricing explores the transformative role of artificial intelligence in modern pricing strategies. The book delves into how AI enhances decision-making, making pricing more proactive, predictive, and personalized. Covering essential AI technologies, case studies, and organizational change management, it provides a comprehensive guide for businesses seeking to integrate AI into their pricing functions. Readers will gain insights into data-driven methodologies, dynamic pricing applications, and future trends shaping AI-powered pricing. The book balances technical depth with practical implementation strategies, making it an invaluable resource for pricing professionals, business leaders, and AI practitioners.

Contents

1   Setting the Stage   1

2   The Building Blocks of AI-Enabled Pricing   15

3   Case Studies: AI in Action   87

4   Guiding Organizational Change for AI-Enabled Pricing   115

5   The Future of AI-Enabled Pricing   131

Appendix: Mastering AI Prompts for Smarter Pricing Advice   143

1

Setting the Stage

Introduction

In the realm of pricing, every decision is very much a delicate balancing act, where strategy, data, intuition, and market dynamics intersect. For decades, pricing professionals have leaned on familiar tools like Excel, staying late to tweak margins, study competitive movements, and assemble fragmented insights. While these methods have been dependable, they are inherently reactive and lack the agility to address today's complex challenges.

Imagine if pricing could transcend these manual processes, becoming proactive, predictive, and tailored to individual customer behaviors. This is where artificial intelligence (AI) enters the picture, not as a distant concept but as a fast-evolving technology already permeating various business practices. AI has the potential to revolutionize pricing strategies, enabling companies to keep abreast of market changes, dynamically adjust prices, and enhance customer experiences with precision. Jeff Bezos (2023) described AI as a "horizontal enabling layer" that improves everything it touches, from business processes to public services.

Despite bright outlook, many professionals still find themselves stuck with static tools, struggling to tackle dynamic challenges with outdated approaches. This reliance not only harms efficiency but also leaves businesses vulnerable in an era that demands agility and data-driven precision.

This chapter sets the stage for understanding how AI is reshaping pricing and taking it to the next level. I will explore the fundamentals of AI-enabled pricing and the broader forces fueling its adoption, from advancements in machine learning to the growing imperative for real-time decision-making.

By the end of this chapter, you will understand why AI is not just a passing trend but a critical evolution in the pricing landscape.

Whether you are a pricing expert seeking to modernize or a business leader searching for strategies to enhance growth, this chapter is your starting point for appreciating AI's transformative power. The future of pricing has arrived, and now is the time to lead the way.

Why Pricing Matters More Than Ever

The Power of Pricing: Beyond the Bottom Line

Pricing, at its core, weaves a compelling narrative that speaks volumes about a product's perceived value, quality, and exclusivity. Every price conveys a message, influencing how customers connect emotionally with the brand. However, the strategic essence of pricing often takes a back seat to routine operations and efforts to gain market share. The pricing power in shaping profitability and brand perception remains underexploited.

A robust pricing strategy crafts a brand's identity. Consider the Hermès Birkin bag, with its astronomical price tag. This is not just a reflection of cost; it underscores a narrative of scarcity, unparalleled craftsmanship, and exclusivity. By steadfastly refusing discounts, Hermès reinforces its luxury positioning and fosters an aspirational allure among its clientele. Compare this to the ubiquitous "50% Off!" signs in retail stores, which mean to signal urgency and accessibility but can dilute a brand's prestige and create an impression of fleeting value.

The Hermès strategy exemplifies a fundamental principle: pricing is strategic. As Martin and Dholakia (2020) emphasize, sustaining consistent pricing discipline avoids eroding customer trust and reinforces long-term brand equity. In stark contrast, brands that rely heavily on discounts often fall into a "promotion trap," where customers grow accustomed to waiting for sales. Research supports this phenomenon, showing that frequent promotions diminish perceived value and foster disloyalty over time (Nagle and Müller 2018).

Modern markets demand that businesses view pricing as more than a transactional tool. It is a strategic lever to navigate increased competition, informed consumers, and the challenges brought by digital innovation. Companies that fail to adapt risk losing their foothold in increasingly volatile markets.

As Dolan and Simon (1996) highlight, disciplined pricing strategies yield consistently superior performance compared to traditional approaches. By integrating pricing as a strategic priority, companies can redefine its role beyond profit maximization. Pricing becomes a medium through which brands express their ethos, ambitions, and unique value proposition to the market, fostering deeper trust, engagement, and loyalty.

Challenges in Traditional Pricing

Pricing is arguably the most significant lever for business success, yet many organizations continue to underutilize its potential. Despite its direct influence on revenue and profitability, traditional methods often fall short in addressing the complexities of today's dynamic and fast-evolving markets. Below, I will go over critical challenges that make conventional pricing approaches insufficient for modern business needs.

Outdated Practices in a Constantly Changing World

Today a lot of businesses remain hostage to static pricing frameworks, such as cost-plus pricing or market benchmarking. While straightforward, these methods are increasingly inadequate in today's volatile economic environment. Cost-plus pricing, for example, puts customer demand on the sidelines, focusing primarily on internal cost structures and wishful goals. Similarly, market benchmarking assumes competitors' pricing strategies are sound, a risky bet in highly competitive and fluid markets.

Consider the case of a mid-sized hotel chain that adhered to fixed seasonal pricing, adjusting rates only twice annually. One summer, a major international sports event unexpectedly brought an influx of travelers to one of their key markets. Competitors using dynamic pricing capitalized on the demand surge, significantly increasing revenue. Meanwhile, the hotel chain, with its static pricing strategy, missed out on substantial revenue potential, demonstrating the limitations of rigid approaches in an unpredictable world.

Businesses cling to these outdated methods because they feel familiar and appear less risky. However, as demand patterns become increasingly influenced by factors like global crises, digital trends, and even viral content, organizations that resist evolving their pricing strategies face the danger of becoming obsolete.

Siloed Data Handling

Effective pricing decisions depend on insights from multiple business functions, such as sales, marketing, supply chain, and finance. In reality, many organizations operate in silos, with each department managing its own data and systems. This fragmented approach poses significant challenges, as pricing requires a holistic view of a range of factors such as costs, competitor actions, and customer demand.

For instance, a wholesale distributor discovered that its pricing team was unknowingly setting prices below acceptable profit margins. Why? The team lacked visibility into updated logistics costs managed by the supply chain department. The result was a disconnect that led to eroded margins, frustrated stakeholders, and lost opportunities to adjust pricing in line with real costs.

Data silos not only hinder effective pricing decisions. Moreover, they delay responses to market changes. Without integrated systems, pricing teams often rely on manual processes to piece together insights, leading to inefficiencies and missed revenue opportunities. Modern organizations need centralized platforms or interconnected tools to break down these silos and provide a unified data source for pricing strategies.

Cognitive Bias in Decision-Making

Even when organizations have access to relevant data, human biases can undermine pricing strategies. It is not uncommon that sales or pricing managers base their decisions on intuition or personal experience, which leads to biases and errors time and again.

A classic example is the fear of alienating customers with price increases. Even when data indicates customers are willing to pay more, pricing or sales teams may hesitate, forgoing deserved revenue opportunities. This tendency to undervalue products or services often stems from a lack of confidence in data-driven insights.

Anchoring bias is another common issue. Decision-makers may fixate on an initial price point based on gut feelings, failing to digest evolving market conditions or customer preferences. This bias can prevent businesses from adjusting prices effectively, resulting in stagnation or a decline in competitiveness.

To overcome these cognitive biases, organizations can integrate AI-enabled tools that provide objective recommendations. By combining human intuition with machine-generated insights, businesses can combine creativity and precision, making pricing decisions that are both strategic and data-informed.

The Painful Time Crunch

One of the most pressing pain points plaguing traditional pricing systems is the immense amount of time needed to manage pricing across multiple products, regions, and channels. Innumerable pricing teams find themselves stuck in a cycle of manual work, updating price lists, reconciling discrepancies, analyzing competitive data, not to mention tedious alignment with different stakeholders. This labor-intensive process leaves little time for strategic initiatives or innovation.

Consider the case of a global distributor managing a portfolio of over 400,000 SKUs. Their pricing team was stretched thin, spending days manually calculating markups and updating spreadsheets. When a competitor launched a disruptive promotion, it took the company nearly 3 weeks to adjust their own pricing strategy. By the time their revised prices hit the market, they had already ceded a significant share to the competitor. Slow reaction times were costly.

The issue is magnified in large organizations, where lengthy approval processes tend to stall pricing decisions. Layers of hierarchy, cross-departmental dependencies, and frequent back-and-forth alignments can turn a seemingly straightforward pricing update into a drawn-out ordeal. For instance, a multinational electronics manufacturer reported that it often took 6–8 weeks to implement price changes globally, as adjustments had to be reviewed, aligned with, and approved by multiple regional and central teams. In such cases, even minor delays can erode competitive advantage and lead to lost revenue opportunities.

Automation and AI technologies offer a superior solution by significantly reducing the manual workload and compressing timelines. Tools powered by machine learning can dynamically update pricing models based on market conditions, customer behavior, and competitor moves in real time. However, companies are likely to resist these tools, clinging to outdated systems simply out of inertia or fear of change.

Breaking free from this time trap demands a change of mindset. Organizations must streamline approval processes, empower pricing teams to make decisions swiftly, and embrace the speed and efficiency that AI-enabled systems provide. By reducing manual workloads and accelerating decision-making, businesses can shift their focus from operational bottlenecks to strategic opportunities, ensuring they stay resilient in today's fast-paced market.

The Call for Change

The limitations of traditional pricing methods present an opportunity for transformation rather than defeat. To seize this opportunity, businesses should move beyond static strategies, dismantle departmental silos, confront ingrained cognitive biases, and adopt forward-thinking technologies like AI and automation. Pricing should be remodeled to a central pillar of strategic innovation and sustainable growth.

Modern markets demand agility and foresight, traits that outdated approaches simply cannot provide. Embracing change means reimagining pricing as a dynamic, data-driven discipline capable of anticipating customer needs, responding to market fluctuations, and unlocking untapped potential.

In the chapters ahead, I will delve into how AI addresses these challenges, transforming pricing into a proactive, predictive, and personalized engine for growth. From optimizing price points in real time to uncovering hidden market opportunities, AI offers tools that enable businesses to outpace competitors while building stronger relationships with customers.

AI's Potential to Revolutionize Pricing

Where does AI fit into the pricing equation? The most compelling aspect is not its ability to fix inefficiencies. It is the way it redefines what pricing can achieve. By using vast datasets and advanced algorithms, AI empowers businesses to adapt, personalize, and predict with unprecedented accuracy. Let's delve into how AI is reshaping the pricing landscape.

Dynamic Pricing in Action

Imagine a pricing system that reacts instantly to real-time conditions, seamlessly adjusting rates based on demand, competitor behavior, and external factors like weather. AI-enabled dynamic pricing makes this vision a reality by processing thousands of variables simultaneously, providing businesses with agility and precision beyond human ability.

Take Elena, a resort manager in Santorini, Greece, as an example. Her team implemented an AI-enabled system to manage room rates. Initially, she had doubts about relinquishing control to algorithms. But the results spoke for themselves: a 12% increase in average daily rates during peak season, all thanks to the AI's ability to adjust prices in real time, responding to booking trends and competitor activity. "It worked like a charm," she said, in awe of how effortlessly the system balanced demand with profitability.

This capability is no longer exclusive to trailblazing industries like e-commerce or travel. Companies across sectors are embracing dynamic pricing powered by AI. For instance, neural networks can process non-linear relationships between variables, unraveling nuanced demand patterns that traditional models often overlook. Retailers use AI to manage pricing for millions of SKUs, capturing value even during fleeting market shifts (Phillips 2005; Bertsimas and Kallus 2020).

Dynamic pricing represents just one piece of AI's transformative potential. Beyond real-time adjustments, AI enables businesses to explore scenarios, predict market behavior, and personalize customer experiences at scale. These capabilities are redefining pricing, turning a historically reactive function into a forward-looking strategic advantage.

As industries continue to adopt AI, its applications in pricing are expected to grow more and more sophisticated, opening doors to innovations we are only beginning to imagine. With the ability to harness complex datasets and adapt on the fly, AI is setting a new standard for what pricing can accomplish in an ever-evolving market.

Personalized Pricing

Personalized pricing has become an integral part of modern business strategies, often working in stealth to enhance customer retention and profitability. Consider this common scenario: You are about to cancel your subscription to a streaming service when, suddenly, you are offered a discount tailored specifically to you. This is not a fluke. It is AI at work, analyzing customer behavior and identifying you as an at-risk user. By stepping in with the right offer at the right time, the platform not only retains your subscription but also strengthens your loyalty.

For businesses, personalized pricing represents a tremendous opportunity. It shifts the paradigm from blanket discounts, which can erode profit margins, to targeted incentives designed to appeal to individual customers. One leading streaming service reported a 20% improvement in retention rates after deploying AI-enabled personalized pricing strategies. The system used customer activity data, such as watch history and subscription patterns, to tailor offers that felt relevant and timely.

This pricing approach unlocks untapped value by catering to varying levels of willingness to pay. Picture an AI system analyzing a customer's purchasing habits, browsing history, and even sentiment in customer service interactions. Using this data, the system crafts tailored pricing that resonates personally, ensuring the customer perceives the price as fair and relevant. As contended by Bertsimas and Kallus (2020), using AI to align pricing with individual customer profiles can significantly enhance both profitability and customer satisfaction. By demonstrating an understanding of individual needs and preferences, companies foster trust and loyalty. This very sense of fairness rooted in pricing strategies would strengthen the customer relationship, positioning the business as a thoughtful partner rather than a faceless entity.

In a marketplace defined by choice and competition, personalized pricing is more a necessity than a luxury. As AI continues to develop, its capacity to offer hyper-personalized experiences will only grow, creating a future where pricing becomes more instrumental in shaping the customer journey.

Predictive Forecasting

Imagine having the power to anticipate future market trends and proactively adjust your pricing strategies to align with them. With AI-enabled predictive forecasting, this vision is becoming a reality. Advanced tools like Facebook Prophet and similar machine learning models analyze historical data, uncover patterns, and forecast demand trends, empowering businesses to transition from reactive to proactive decision-making.

Consider Walmart's innovative use of AI through its system, Eden. Eden adjusts inventory for perishable goods by analyzing variables such as temperature, humidity, and product quality. This system has helped Walmart significantly reduce waste and improve operational efficiency. Over 5 years, this predictive approach reportedly saved the company $2 billion, underscoring the immense value of AI-powered forecasting in driving financial and operational performance (Marr 2018).

Similarly, H&M has applied predictive forecasting to revolutionize its inventory management. Partnering with Google Cloud, the retailer integrated AI models to analyze sales trends, customer preferences, and external factors like weather or local events. This helped H&M better align product availability with customer demand, reducing unsold inventory and supporting sustainability goals by minimizing waste (Chitrakorn 2020).

Predictive forecasting goes beyond inventory management. It enables businesses to adjust pricing dynamically in response to anticipated shifts in demand. For example, an airline could forecast seasonal travel peaks and offer promotions early to maximize bookings, while a retailer might adjust discounts based on projected buying behavior during the holiday season. These advance adjustments help optimize revenue while enhancing customer satisfaction by ensuring timely and relevant offers.

From a strategic point of view, predictive forecasting can transform businesses into agile, market-responsive entities. By employing AI to predict demand fluctuations, companies can achieve a delicate balance between maximizing profitability and delivering exceptional customer experiences. As these tools advance, they will reshape industries, establishing new benchmarks for strategic, data-driven decision-making.

Pricing Scenarios Made Easy

Pricing professionals have always been dreaming about a pricing crystal ball. AI may turn out to be the closest thing to it. Generative AI, for example, with its advanced modeling capabilities, is enabling businesses to simulate and evaluate pricing strategies across a variety of hypothetical scenarios, providing a roadmap for navigating uncertainty.

Consider the case of a prominent retailer gearing up for a potential price war. Through AI-powered scenario modeling, the company examined the implications of increasing its prices by 5% while a competitor slashed theirs by 10%. The simulation revealed that focusing on loyal customers with targeted value-added promotions, rather than across-the-board discounts, could mitigate potential losses while retaining market share. This insight allowed the retailer to maintain profitability without being drawn into blindsided discounting battles.

Scenario modeling also shines when dealing with external disruptions. For instance, AI can simulate the impacts of supply chain bottlenecks or sudden economic downturns. Businesses gain clarity on how variables like fluctuating material costs or shifting consumer behavior could influence pricing outcomes. This approach not only supports operational continuity but also helps capture opportunities to enhance resilience in uncertain markets (Hinterhuber and Liozu 2013).

One manufacturing firm used AI to simulate how varying raw material costs would impact their production expenses over a 3-month period. The AI model revealed potential savings by prioritizing certain suppliers and suggested a price increase threshold that would not alienate price-sensitive customers. This level of foresight enabled the business to act decisively, strengthening its market position while navigating volatile conditions.

Generative AI's ability to craft detailed "what-if" scenarios holds the potential to refine how businesses approach pricing strategy. By understanding the consequences of various actions before they unfold, companies can shift from reactive measures to proactive, strategic decision-making. This capability does not just reduce risk but also opens doors to innovative approaches that drive long-term success.

Listening to the Market's Pulse

Understanding customer sentiment has always been crucial in shaping pricing strategies, but AI has revolutionized the way how businesses can "listen" to their audiences. By analyzing vast amounts of unstructured data, including online reviews, social media discussions, and customer complaints, AI offers actionable insights into consumer perceptions of price fairness and value.

For example, a leading beauty brand "eavesdropped" on social media conversations about its products with help of Generative AI, which found a growing willingness among customers to pay a premium for items with sustainable packaging. Armed with this insight, the company introduced a tiered pricing structure for eco-friendly lines, increasing profitability by 12% while enhancing its reputation as an environmentally conscious brand. This strategic pivot resonated deeply with eco-aware consumers, leading to greater loyalty and a broader customer base.

AI's real-time capabilities make it a game changer in adapting pricing strategies. During a product launch, for instance, a beverage company used AI to gauge sentiment around its pricing in different regions. By analyzing customer tweets and reviews, the AI revealed that customers in urban areas viewed the price as fair, while rural consumers expressed concerns about affordability. This feedback allowed the company to introduce localized pricing, addressing regional disparities without losing its grip on the broader customer base.

In addition, AI uncovers the emotional drivers influencing consumer behavior. For example, sentiment analysis tools can detect whether customers perceive a price increase as a reflection of improved quality or as an exploitative move. This nuanced understanding ensures pricing adjustments meet consumer expectations, reducing the risk of backlash while maximizing profitability (Tene and Polonetsky 2013).

By integrating AI into pricing strategies, businesses can respond quickly to shifts in market sentiment, ensuring their pricing reflects real-time customer values. This approach not only bolsters customer satisfaction but also fortifies brand trust in an increasingly competitive landscape.

The Transformative Potential of AI in Pricing

Artificial intelligence is fundamentally reshaping pricing strategies. From enabling real-time price adjustments and hyper-personalized offers to uncovering predictive insights and analyzing market sentiment, AI provides businesses with unprecedented tools to make informed, agile, and customer-centric pricing decisions.

What makes AI truly transformative is its ability to merge the precision of data analytics with the nuanced understanding of human behavior and market fluctuations. Traditional pricing rested on static models and historical data. AI, however, introduces a dynamic element, allowing businesses to respond to real-time changes and anticipate future trends. For example, companies can use reinforcement learning to optimize pricing dynamically in industries like retail and ride-sharing, while Generative AI helps simulate market scenarios to test pricing strategies before execution.

AI also transcends numbers to address the psychological aspects of pricing. By analyzing customer preferences, willingness to pay, and sentiment, businesses can craft strategies that resonate on an emotional level. This humanized approach drives revenue, while fostering trust and loyalty.

For organizations ready to explore the possibilities, AI is nothing less than a revolutionary force. By uniting the science of advanced algorithms with the art of understanding customer needs, AI enables businesses to stay competitive in a fast-changing world. Meanwhile, AI-enabled pricing is about creating intelligent, adaptable systems that empower businesses to thrive.

Pricing Remains Human-Driven

I deliberately use "AI-enabled" and "AI-powered" throughout this book rather than "AI-driven." This distinction is not just semantics. It underlines my fundamental belief of how technology should intersect with pricing.

At the end of the day, pricing remains an inherently human activity. It is about understanding people, i.e., your customers, your market, and the values that drive your business. Pricing, as a yardstick for value exchange, requires balancing profitability with fairness, aligning decisions with your company's mission. No matter how sophisticated, AI cannot replicate the empathy and nuance that human judgment brings to these decisions. No matter how powerful a tool AI is, it does not replace human involvement; rather, it levels up the pricing game.

In fact, AI's true strength lies not in taking over decision-making, but in making us better decision-makers. AI can process and analyze vast quantities of data that humans simply cannot keep up with. It reveals patterns, offers predictive insights, and takes over mundane tasks, allowing us to focus on the bigger picture. But when it comes to determining the value of a product, understanding customer sentiment, and aligning decisions with broader business or societal values, this is where the human touch remains irreplaceable yet.

Take, for example, a German technology company that implemented AI-enabled pricing models for its subscription services. While the system optimized prices in real time, based on competitor movements, demand patterns, and seasonality, the marketing team continued to assume a crucial role in shaping special promotions. The AI produced valuable insights, but it was the team's human judgment that ensured the promotions fit with customer expectations and the brand's identity. When a competitor slashed prices unexpectedly, the AI suggested lowering their prices as well. However, the team decided to launch a loyalty campaign instead, offering added value through premium services, which helped nurturing customer trust and preserved their pricing structure.

AI, as a horizontal enabling layer, helps pricing professionals make more informed, efficient, and strategic choices. The combination of human intuition (or empathy at times) with AI's data processing power creates a refined pricing strategy that is both customer-centric and aligned with business goals.

References

Bertsimas D, Kallus N (2020) From predictive to prescriptive analytics. Manag Sci 66(3):1025–1044. https://doi.org/10.1287/mnsc.2018.3253

Bezos J (2023) Machine learning and AI as horizontal enabling layers. Retail Dive. Retrieved from https://www.retaildive.com

Chitrakorn K (2020) How H&M is betting on artificial intelligence to boost its fortunes. Vogue Business. Retrieved from https://www.voguebusiness.com

Dolan RJ, Simon H (1996) Power pricing: how managing price transforms the bottom line. Free Press

Hinterhuber A, Liozu SM (2013) Innovation in pricing: contemporary theories and best practices. Routledge

Marr B (2018) How Walmart is using machine learning, AI, and big data to boost performance. Forbes. Retrieved from https://www.forbes.com

Martin KD, Dholakia UM (2020) Fostering customer trust through ethical AI practices. J Bus Ethics 163(4):705–718. https://doi.org/10.1007/s10551-019-04360-4

Nagle TT, Müller G (2018) The strategy and tactics of pricing: A guide to growing more profitably, 6th edn. Routledge

Phillips R (2005) Pricing and revenue optimization. Stanford Business Books

Tene O, Polonetsky J (2013) Big data for all: Privacy and user control in the age of analytics. Nw J Tech Intell Prop 11(5):239–273. https://doi.org/10.2139/ssrn.2149369

2

The Building Blocks of AI-Enabled Pricing

Introduction

Imagine you are building a skyscraper. Every decision you make, from laying the foundation to completing the top floor, must be carefully calculated, based on precise measurements and a solid plan. The same principle applies to AI-enabled pricing. Before you can create a system that improves pricing decisions, it is essential to ensure that all foundational elements are set in place.

In this chapter, I will examine the core building blocks that comprise and power AI pricing systems. From the data that fuels the algorithms to the AI models and the end-to-end processes that generate pricing recommendations, each component is crucial in making AI a valuable and effective tool for your business. In sum, I want to offer a holistic view on how to effectively utilize data and technology to accomplish your business goals and deliver tangible, measurable outcomes.

You may have heard the saying "garbage in, garbage out," which is just as true for AI in pricing. Without high-quality data, even the most sophisticated AI models will not be able to generate valuable insights. When the right building blocks come together, however, the potential for transformation is immense. AI can predict demand, optimize pricing in real-time, and personalize offers in ways that were previously unthinkable.

In this chapter, I will explore how to establish that foundation, choose the appropriate models, navigate the challenges of integrating AI into your pricing strategy, and lastly, institutionalize AI-enabled pricing in the organization. The journey ahead may appear challenging, but with the right foundation in place, the possibilities are limitless.

Data: The Fuel for AI in Pricing

In the world of pricing, the balance between value and profitability or any other goal tandems is a delicate art, and data serves as the essential tool that shapes this process. Just as an artist needs the right colors to create a masterpiece, a business requires the right data to craft an effective pricing strategy. Without it, your pricing decisions may lack direction or fail to achieve their intended outcomes. While AI has the potential to induce significant improvements, its effectiveness is directly tied to the quality of the data it uses. The "garbage in, garbage out" principle underlines the importance of reliable and accurate data in AI pricing (Marr 2018).

But what types of data are critical for AI-enabled pricing? How do you obtain and process this data? And how do you transform raw, often messy data into valuable, actionable insights? In this section, I will delve into the foundational role that data plays in AI-enabled pricing strategies, providing insight into how businesses can leverage data effectively to maximize the benefits of AI (Binns 2021; Davenport and Ronanki 2018).

Identifying and Collecting Relevant Pricing Data

Embarking on an AI-enabled pricing strategy means embracing a vast amount of data. With such an abundance of information at their fingertips, pricing professionals might get data-sick and wonder where to start. The key is not about gathering every piece of data but rather identifying the data that is most relevant to pricing decisions. In this section, I will focus on four types of data that are central to building a successful AI pricing strategy.

Transactional Data: The Foundation of Insights

At the core of AI-enabled pricing lies transactional data like sales history, quantities sold, timestamps, and invoice records. This data offers an invaluable snapshot of past behaviors in the marketplace and is one of the most direct ways to understand customer purchasing patterns. Through the analysis of transactional data, businesses can factor actual demand into their pricing strategies.

Transactional data provides the essential "what" and "when," which in turn can help forecast the "how much" and "at what price." For example, a major consumer goods company reviewed years of sales data to figure out how their high-end and low-end products responded to price changes. They discovered that demand for their premium products was less sensitive to price increases compared to their budget lines. Consequently, the company adjusted its pricing strategy by raising prices for premium items while keeping budget-friendly options competitive. In just six months, they saw an 8% increase in overall profits (EY 2023b).

Smaller businesses can equally benefit from transactional data. A bakery in Seattle, for instance, saw a seasonal spike in cupcake sales each December. Initially thought to be a random occurrence, further analysis showed that corporate holiday orders were the primary driver. By offering bulk discounts to local businesses, the bakery saw a 25% increase in December sales, proving the power of even basic transactional data in driving growth.

The strength of transactional data is rooted in its ability to reveal subtle patterns that might not be immediately apparent. This type of data can uncover seasonal fluctuations, identify top-performing products, and pinpoint purchasing habits that suggest when customers are willing to pay premium prices. For instance, a consumer electronics retailer used transactional data to predict peak demand periods for gaming consoles. By adjusting their pricing strategy to reflect these trends, offering slight discounts during off-peak times and raising prices as demand surges, they optimized inventory turnover and profit margins.

However, the insights derived from transactional data depend heavily on the quality of the data itself. Raw data is often fragmented, scattered across various systems, and prone to inconsistencies and noises. Common issues include gaps in pricing history, duplicate entries, or varying formats across platforms. Companies must invest in consolidating their data sources and ensuring accuracy before feeding it into AI systems. Once cleaned and enriched, transactional data can become one of the most powerful sources for pricing managers, offering actionable insights that are deeply aligned with customer behavior.

With transactional data serving as a foundational element, companies can build AI-enabled pricing strategies that are both precise and adaptable. Whether optimizing margins, understanding price sensitivity, or predicting demand peaks, the insights from transactional data offer unparalleled clarity and can translate raw records into strategic intelligence.

Customer Behavior Data: Uncovering the "Why"

While transactional data reveals the "what" of customer behavior, customer behavior data digs deeper, decoding the "why" behind these actions. This data offers a window into customer motivations, preferences, and decision-making processes. It includes details such as browsing patterns, time spent on specific product pages, cart abandonment rates, and metrics related to customer loyalty. By incorporating this data into pricing strategies, businesses can move away from generic, one-size-fits-all models and toward more personalized, dynamic approaches.

Consider the case of a fitness app that tracked user behavior. The app's data revealed that while a decent number of users explored its premium subscription plans, very few were making the final purchase. The company dove deeper into the data, looking at session lengths, click paths, and where users dropped off in the subscription process. This analysis led to a targeted campaign offering hesitant users a $5 discount on their first month. The results were immediate, with a 15% increase in conversions, offering the company valuable insights into the factors influencing customer decisions (Emerald Insight 2023a, b).

Understanding the "why" behind customer behavior cultivates new insights. For example, browsing patterns can reveal which products or price points attract attention but fail to convert, creating opportunities to refine product positioning. Cart abandonment rates often point to issues with price sensitivity or perceived value at checkout. Additionally, loyalty metrics help businesses evaluate which pricing strategies resonate with repeat customers, providing a robust foundation for refining long-term pricing policies.

In another case, an online fashion retailer noticed a high rate of cart abandonment linked to expensive shipping fees. By deciphering behavior data, the company implemented a strategy offering free shipping for orders above a specific threshold. In addition to reducing abandonment, this approach boosted average order values by 20%, showing the impact of using customer behavior data to refine pricing (McKinsey and Company 2023).

Customer behavior data turned out to be a gold mine for a SaaS company providing multiple subscription tier. They found that a substantial number of free-tier users explored premium features without upgrading in the end. The company responded by offering a limited-time trial to unlock all features for free-tier users. Following the trial, personalized pricing offers based on usage patterns resulted in a 25% increase in upgrades within a quarter, demonstrating the value of aligning pricing with customer behavior.

Real-time adjustments are another advantage elicited from behavior data. Social media activity can signal shifts in customer sentiment, allowing businesses to quickly adapt their promotions or pricing. For example, a beauty brand noticed a surge in searches and site visits after an influencer reviewed one of their products. Seizing the opportunity, the company launched a flash sale, channeling the spike in interest into immediate sales.

While transactional data shows past behaviors, customer behavior data reveals the underlying thought process behind those actions. It helps businesses answer some tricky questions: Why do some customers hesitate to purchase? What drives repeat purchases? What factors cause customers to abandon their carts? By connecting these insights, companies can refine their pricing strategies to better satisfy customer needs and expectations, delivering value that feels intuitive and personalized.

Incorporating behavior data into pricing strategies does not just lead to higher revenue but also builds trust and fosters loyalty at the same time. When customers see that their individual preferences are reflected in pricing offers, it creates a sense of fairness and transparency. Over time, this approach transforms static pricing strategies into adaptive, customer-centric systems that continuously evolve based on real-time data and customer insights.

Market Trend Data: Adapting to External Forces

Market trend data plays a crucial role in ensuring that pricing strategies remain relevant and adaptive in a constantly shifting environment. Unlike transactional or behavior data, which focus on individual customer actions, market trend data factors in broader external influences such as economic shifts, weather conditions, and cultural trends. These insights allow businesses to adjust their pricing in response to factors beyond their immediate control, ensuring they stay competitive and aligned with current market realities.

For example, a ski resort in Colorado strategically adjusted its ticket prices based on weather forecasts. When heavy snowfalls were expected, indicating increased demand for skiing, they raised prices to get abreast of the surge in visitors. On sunnier, snowless weekends, they lowered prices to attract hesitant customers, optimizing revenue during peak times and ensuring a steady stream of visitors during quieter periods. By adapting their pricing strategy in response to external factors, they managed to boost profitability while keeping their customer base engaged (KDnuggets 2023a).

Market trend data also reveals potential opportunities that may not be immediately apparent. A global footwear brand, for instance, took an opportunity at an international sporting event to drive sales. Noticing a surge in interest in a specific sport, they raised prices for limited-edition items while launching well-timed promotions for standard products, resulting in a 17% increase in sales over the course of the event. This strategy helped the company capitalize on cultural moments and offer both exclusive and accessible pricing options.

The adaptability of market trend data extends across industries. For instance, a restaurant chain responded to rising inflation by adjusting its pricing strategy using macroeconomic data. They introduced smaller portions at lower prices (note the difference from shrinkflation) and bundled high-margin items with customer favorites to ensure affordability without sacrificing profitability. This approach allowed them to defend their competitive edge in challenging times by making pricing more adaptable to the economic climate.

Similarly, retailers routinely use market trend data to adjust their pricing according to consumer sentiment during special occasions. A gift shop chain, for example, used insights about Mother's Day shopping habits to implement dynamic discounts, offering larger discounts earlier and tapering off closer to the holiday. This strategy encouraged early purchases while still capturing late buyers at premium prices, optimizing both timing and sales volume.

Market trend data is also instrumental in preparing for unpredictable events. Airlines, for example, adjust their fares based on fluctuations in oil prices. When fuel costs rise, airlines use market data to apply incremental surcharges, maintaining profitability without shocking customers with dramatic price hikes. Conversely, when fuel prices fall, these insights allow airlines to offer discounts that drive bookings.

The integration of AI into the analysis of market trend data further fortifies its prowess. AI algorithms can process vast datasets, detecting patterns that would be difficult for humans to discern. For example, a global logistics company combined market trend data with AI to predict supply chain disruptions caused by extreme weather. By dynamically adjusting pricing based on anticipated demand spikes, the company optimized revenue while keeping customers satisfied.

The beauty of market trend data lies in its potential to enable businesses to be proactive rather than reactive. By embracing external insights, companies can transform uncertainty into opportunity, aligning their pricing strategies with seasonal shifts, economic conditions, and cultural moments. This approach not only ensures that pricing is responsive and relevant but also fosters customer trust by providing value in every transaction.

Overcoming Data Challenges

Collecting the right data is a crucial first step in leveraging AI for pricing. However, this process is often overwhelming. Raw data is typically fragmented, messy, and voluminous, presenting significant challenges for businesses. Even the most advanced AI systems are only as effective as the data they are built on, making data management a fundamental step. Addressing these issues early on is key to ensuring that AI-enabled pricing decisions are robust, actionable, and valuable for business grow.

Ensuring Data Quality

Without reliable data, even the most advanced AI algorithms cannot yield valuable insights. Inaccurate, incomplete, or inconsistent data can distort predictions, leading to poor pricing decisions. For example, a retailer that adjusts prices with flawed data during peak holiday seasons could either overcharge customers for in-demand products or miss opportunities to capitalize on spikes in demand.

Maintaining adequate data quality may not be the most glamorous aspect of pricing, but it is undeniably essential. Cleaning data entails tasks such as removing duplicates, addressing missing entries, and standardizing formats. One common issue arises when different systems record data in varying formats, such as date and price formats. For instance, one platform might use the decimal point ($39.99) while another uses the decimal comma ($39,99), leading to nasty hiccups during analysis. A global retailer experienced this when inconsistencies in data formats led to erroneous pricing recommendations, causing both lost revenue and dissatisfied customers.

Tools such as Python's pandas library can help automate and simplify this process, even for large datasets. By ensuring the accuracy and consistency of data, businesses can lay a solid foundation for their AI-enabled pricing strategies, making sure that insights derived from the data are both reliable and actionable. Here is how businesses can approach cleaning data:

```
import pandas as pd

# Load messy data
df = pd.read_csv('pricing_data.csv')

# Remove duplicates
df = df.drop_duplicates()

# Convert decimal commas to decimal points in the
'price' column
if df['price'].dtype == 'object':   # Check if the column contains strings
    df['price'] = df['price'].str.replace(',', '.',
    regex=False)
```

```
# Convert the 'price' column to numeric
df['price'] = pd.to_numeric(df['price'], errors='coerce')

# Fill missing prices with the average
df['price'] = df['price'].fillna(df['price'].mean())

print("Cleaned Data:", df.head())
```

Taking the time to clean and standardize data is a worthwhile investment, as it sets a sturdy foundation for AI models. Although it may seem tedious, this process is vital for ensuring the accuracy of the insights generated by AI systems and for fostering trust in the technology, preventing costly errors in decision-making. One common issue that organizations face is fragmented data. Businesses often operate with siloed systems across departments like sales, marketing, inventory, and finance, with limited integration. These silos make it challenging to create a comprehensive dataset that reflects the entire customer journey. For instance, the sales team may track transactions, while the marketing team tracks promotion performance, but neither has access to the other's data. Integrating these disparate sources is like solving a complex puzzle, while the payoff is the much-needed ability to generate more precise and complete pricing insights.

A consumer electronics company encountered this issue when its online and in-store sales data were managed separately. This fragmentation resulted in disjointed pricing strategies. By consolidating the data into a unified platform, the company uncovered an interesting trend: flash sales performed better online, while steady discounts were more effective for in-store customers. This insight allowed them to tailor their pricing strategies according to the sales channel, increasing revenue.

Managing data volume is another challenge in today's data-rich world. With the vast amount of data available, businesses can easily become overwhelmed or focus on irrelevant metrics. AI thrives on large datasets, but simply having more data is not always better. Efficiently processing large datasets requires scalable tools such as Apache Spark or cloud platforms like AWS and Azure. To avoid being inundated with data, businesses should consciously prioritize quality over quantity. Focusing on the most impactful datasets, such as sales history and customer behavior, allows companies to start small and scale as the system matures. This approach makes the process more manageable while ensuring that the initial insights are actionable and relevant.

Overcoming these challenges does not equate to solving technical problems. It comes down to cultivating a culture of data-driven decision-making. By investing in clean, consolidated, and high-quality data, businesses can create a solid foundation for AI-powered pricing strategies that deliver tangible results. Admittedly, the effort required may be considerable. The rewards such as accurate insights, optimized margins, and a competitive edge are well worth it. With the right data infrastructure, companies can turn their data into a strategic asset, transforming pricing from an art into a science.

Integrating Disparate Data Sources

Merging data across organizational silos is like forcing puzzle pieces from different sets to fit together. Each department, whether it is sales, marketing, inventory, or the supply chain, manages its data in distinct systems with different structures, definitions, granularities, and formats. This siloed approach depicts a biased picture, making it challenging to develop cohesive pricing strategies. It is imperative to find a practical solution to these integration challenges for businesses that wish to fully embrace AI-powered pricing models and data-driven decision-making.

Take, for example, a retailer managing both online and in-store sales operations. Initially, the teams worked independently, each focusing on their respective data streams. The online team tracked website traffic and conversion rates, while the in-store team monitored footfall and shelf placement. Without collaboration or shared insights, these two data streams existed in parallel, never intersecting. It was not until the retailer decided to merge these datasets that a significant trend appeared: flash sales were far more effective online, while in-store customers responded better to smaller, consistent discounts. This insight enabled the retailer to adapt its pricing strategy across both channels, increasing profitability and customer engagement (Microsoft Azure 2023).

Unfortunately, integrating data is not as simple as merging files from different systems. Each department typically uses different formats or definitions for tracking key metrics. For example, one department might track revenue by calendar month, while another uses fiscal quarters. These discrepancies need to be resolved to create a unified dataset that aligns with the organization's overall goals. Although this process can be time-consuming and complex, the benefits are substantial and long-lasting.

Modern data integration platforms like Snowflake and AWS present themselves as useful tools. Snowflake enables seamless data sharing across departments, offering a centralized hub where data from sales, marketing, and inventory can be easily integrated. Similarly, AWS provides scalable infrastructure that can navigate the complexities of merging large datasets, ensuring that businesses can maintain accurate, consistent data as a cohesive whole even as it grows.

Successful data integration relies on a collaborative mindset across teams. Teams must be willing to break down silos and align their objectives to ensure that the data tells a consistent story. For example, a consumer goods company organized cross-departmental workshops to standardize key metrics such as sales velocity and promotional effectiveness. This collaborative effort led to both a unified dataset and a shared understanding of success across the business.

The benefits of integration extend beyond just pricing. By feeding data into a single, comprehensive data hub, businesses gain richer insights, enabling more refined strategies. For example, an electronics retailer merged inventory data with sales trends to anticipate product shortages during peak seasons. By adjusting prices and restocking in advance, they avoided stockouts, ensuring customer satisfaction while maximizing revenue.

Despite all advantages, data integration can turn out to be an unnerving task. Legacy systems often lack the capabilities for seamless data sharing, requiring workarounds or upgrades to facilitate smooth communication. Modern tools may ease technical integration. Nevertheless, cultural resistance within the organization often impedes progress. Teams that are used to operating in silos may be reluctant to share data, fearing a loss of control or authority. Overcoming these barriers requires clear communication about the benefits of integration, both for the company's success and for the individual goals of each department.

Integrating disparate data sources is undoubtedly a complex process, but the rewards are significant. A unified dataset empowers businesses to develop more accurate pricing models and promotes a culture of collaboration and data-driven decision-making. When executed effectively, data integration turns isolated, fragmented pieces into a complete, cohesive picture, providing businesses with the clarity to thrive in competitive, fast-evolving markets.

Managing Data Volume

Managing large datasets for AI-enabled pricing strategies is similar to navigating through a dense, overgrown jungle. While the potential to leverage vast amounts of data is exciting, it is important to remember that more data does not guarantee better outcomes, especially if that data is unstructured, redundant, or irrelevant. The tricky question lies in harnessing high volumes of data while maintaining system efficiency and ensuring that insights stay actionable (Liu et al. 2018).

Tools like Apache Spark and Snowflake are useful for processing and managing large datasets. Apache Spark, for instance, can analyze terabytes of data in parallel, making it invaluable for businesses with expansive datasets. On the other hand, Snowflake's cloud infrastructure provides on-demand scalability, allowing businesses to manage surges in data volume with ease. By using these tools, companies can turn potentially overwhelming data streams into manageable and insightful resources (Bae et al. 2023).

However, the possibility to handle large volumes of data does not mean that businesses should do so at any cost. Starting small is beneficial for keeping focus and clarity. A smaller, more targeted dataset often delivers more actionable insights than a sprawling, disorganized one. For instance, a global retailer focused on sales data from its top-performing regions during its AI pilot phase. This approach allowed the company to refine its algorithms and achieve measurable success before expanding its AI models to other markets (Emerald Insight 2023a, b).

Managing data can be compared with cultivating a garden. If you plant everything at once, it can become overwhelming, resulting in uneven results. By focusing on a few high-impact datasets initially, such as sales transactions and customer behavior, businesses can create a powerful foundation for future, more complex analyses. Over time, they can gradually incorporate broader data, like market trends and competitive intelligence, as the system matures (Liu et al. 2018).

Another key consideration is ensuring that the insights derived from the data are practical and relevant. Too much data can lead to analysis paralysis, where decision-makers become overwhelmed by options. For example, focusing on niche product segments with low sales can distract teams from more critical insights that directly affect pricing strategies. Staying focused on the data that drives business decisions ensures that AI efforts are effective and not bogged down by unnecessary complexity (Jain and Sharma 2021). Even with the best tools in place, large datasets inherently introduce technical challenges. Storage costs, processing speeds, and system compatibility must be considered early on.

In the end, managing data volume is not just about technology. More often, it requires strategic thinking. Understanding when to scale up and when to focus on the most impactful datasets is what distinguishes successful AI initiatives from those that get weighed down by excessive data. By using scalable tools and prioritizing high-value datasets, businesses can transform big data into a strategic asset, enabling smarter, more efficient pricing strategies and offering a competitive edge in an increasingly data-driven landscape.

Why It Matters After All

Data tells the story of your business. Each transaction, click, and abandoned cart is a piece of that story, waiting to be analyzed and understood. Artificial Intelligence (AI) offers the tools needed to decode these narratives, but the story's clarity and accuracy depend entirely on the quality and relevance of the data fed into the system. Collecting data is not enough; it must be curated, refined, and aligned with business objectives to be effective (Chen et al. 2020).

Think of your data as the raw ingredients needed for a gourmet meal. Even the most skilled chef cannot create a masterpiece with spoiled or mismatched ingredients. Similarly, an AI model cannot deliver valuable insights if it is working with fragmented, inconsistent, or irrelevant data. Ensuring that your data is clean and structured is essential to setting the stage for AI to perform at its best.

The importance of cleaning up messy data cannot be overstated. For example, a mid-sized retailer experienced this firsthand. After launching an AI-powered pricing tool, the retailer discovered that its predictions were inaccurate. The problem stemmed from duplicate entries and inconsistent formatting across their datasets. By investing time and resources into cleaning the data and standardizing it, the pricing tool began to provide actionable insights that improved the company's decision-making. This initial setback became a key factor in their success, underscoring the value of properly prepared data.

Experience shows that the difficulty in integrating disparate data sources is often underestimated. Innumerable companies struggle with siloed data, where different departments such as sales, marketing, and inventory rely on their own systems, which do not communicate with each other. Integrating these systems may be like solving a complex puzzle, but the payoff is immense. For example, a logistics company integrated data from its fleet management and customer orders, revealing a critical insight: delayed deliveries were influencing customer price sensitivity. By aligning pricing with delivery schedules, the company improved customer satisfaction and maintained steady revenue, even during peak demand (KDnuggets 2023b).

Data volume has been growing exponentially in today's digital age. Businesses generate vast amounts of data, but not all of it is useful for pricing decisions. It is wise to focus on the most impactful datasets. A global electronics retailer, for example, started its AI pricing initiative by concentrating on two primary metrics, namely sales history and competitor pricing. This targeted approach enabled the company to achieve quick wins, build confidence in the system, and then scale the model to handle more complex data (Emerald Insight 2023a, b).

Why does this all matter? Only by overcoming these challenges, can businesses unlock the full potential of their data. Clean, integrated, and well-managed datasets lay the foundation for AI systems that deliver actionable insights. These systems enable businesses to move from reactive adjustments to proactive strategies, prepare for customer needs and market trends before they happen.

Investing in quality data also builds trust within your organization and with your customers. When employees see that AI systems are based on reliable, high-quality data, they are more likely to embrace them. Customers, too, notice when pricing feels fair and personalized, which fosters a sense of transparency and loyalty. The next section will delve into how AI technologies transform raw data into actionable pricing strategies, enabling smarter and more competitive pricing decisions (Chen et al. 2020).

AI Technologies Revolutionizing Pricing

AI has revolutionized pricing, transitioning it from a reactive function to a proactive, strategic discipline. In the past, pricing decisions were often based on intuition, manual calculations, or rigid rules. Today, AI has empowered businesses to move beyond these traditional methods, allowing them to predict trends, personalize strategies, and adjust in real time. As a result, pricing is not only more precise but also dynamic and aligned with customer needs.

At the core of this paradigm shift are advanced algorithms and innovative technologies. Foundational tools such as Machine Learning (ML) and Natural Language Processing (NLP) form the foundation of predictive analytics and customer sentiment analysis. Meanwhile, Generative AI (Gen AI) and Reinforcement Learning (RL) go even further, introducing a new level of creativity and adaptability to pricing strategies. These technologies are already integral in shaping how companies in industries like retail, travel, and subscription services approach pricing (Brynjolfsson and McAfee 2017; Lee et al. 2021).

The field of AI continues to progress with exciting advancements that expand the possibilities of pricing strategies. For instance, Explainable AI (XAI) is tackling trust, one of the major hindrances in AI adoption, by making the decision-making process behind AI models more transparent. This ensures that pricing decisions can be justified not only to internal stakeholders but also to customers (Gilpin et al. 2018). Additionally, Synthetic Data

Generation allows companies to train AI models without the limitations of incomplete or sensitive datasets, addressing privacy concerns while bolstering robust model performance (Choi et al. 2021). Techniques like Low Rank Adaptation (LoRA) make it easier to fine-tune AI models for specific pricing situations, even with limited computational resources.

Together, these technologies all together give rise to a powerful ecosystem that is transforming the pricing landscape. They empower businesses to efficiently experiment, innovate, and adapt to market shifts in ways that were previously unimaginable. In the following sections, I will take inventory of these technologies, exploring how they function, their practical applications, and the unique advantages they bring to pricing strategies. Whether you are a seasoned pricing expert or new to AI, these tools provide a glimpse into the future of more intelligent and flexible decision-making.

Machine Learning (ML): Predictive Analytics and Price Optimization

Machine Learning (ML) forms the foundation of AI-enabled pricing strategies, offering a dynamic approach to pricing that traditional models cannot match. Unlike conventional statistical models that rely on fixed relationships and produce static predictions, ML adapts to changing market conditions, detecting hidden patterns, and allowing businesses to adjust their pricing strategies in real time to improve both revenue and customer satisfaction (Bertsimas and Kallus 2020).

Simply put, ML processes vast amounts of data into meaningful insights. It does not simply crunch numbers. Instead, it disentangles the intricate relationships between factors like demand, competition, seasonality, and customer preferences. In contrast to static models that depend on predefined assumptions, ML models continuously evolve with the arrival of new data, making them well-suited for today's fast-moving market environments (Choi et al. 2021).

A main application of ML in pricing is predictive pricing. For example, ML models can forecast demand fluctuations, enabling businesses to adjust prices accordingly, thereby maximizing revenue while minimizing costly outcomes such as stockouts or overstocking. Consider a retail business preparing for the holiday season. Instead of relying on guesswork, they use ML to analyze past sales data, predict which items will experience spikes in demand, and set their prices accordingly. This approach ensures well-balanced inventory, higher sales, and satisfied customers (Chen and Zhao 2019).

Another powerful use case of ML is price elasticity analysis. By analyzing how price changes affect consumer demand, ML helps businesses spot the optimal pricing point where they can maximize revenue without alienating price-sensitive customers. For example, a beverage company used ML to find that a 3% price increase on their premium line would have negligible effect on demand while significantly boosting their profit margins (Datamatics 2024).

Retailers also employ ML for dynamic bundling, which identifies frequently purchased product combinations and offers and suggests optimized pricing for these bundles. An e-commerce platform, for instance, noticed that customers often bought wireless headphones alongside phone cases. By bundling these items and offering a slight discount, the platform increased the average order value by 20%, creating a beneficial situation for both the business and its customers (Johnson et al. 2020).

The impact of ML on pricing is rapidly unfolding in the real world. For instance, an international fashion retailer applied ML to forecast demand for seasonal apparel by analyzing historical sales data, current trends, and weather forecasts. By adjusting their pricing strategy based on these predictions, they experienced a 15% increase in seasonal revenue, showing how ML can turn predictive insights into profitable outcomes (EY 2023a).

Technical Insight

ML's predictive power often starts with regression models, which are particularly effective for price optimization. These models analyze relationships between variables like demand, costs, and competitor prices to predict the optimal price point for a product. Below is an example of how this works in Python:

```
from sklearn.linear_model import LinearRegression
from sklearn.model_selection import train_test_split
import pandas as pd

# Load data
data = pd.read_csv("pricing_data.csv")
X = data[['demand', 'competitor_price', 'cost']]
y = data['optimal_price']

# Train/test split
X_train, X_test, y_train, y_test = train_test_split(X, y,
test_size=0.2, random_state=42)
```

```
# Train the regression model
model = LinearRegression()
model.fit(X_train, y_train)

# Predict prices
predicted_prices = model.predict(X_test)
print("Predicted Prices:", predicted_prices)
```

This simple regression model offers a glimpse into how businesses can forecast prices based on key variables. As more data comes in, the model improves, allowing it to evolve abreast with emerging trends and market conditions.

Looking Ahead

ML's role in pricing keeps evolving. Beyond predictive pricing, elasticity analysis, and bundling, advanced techniques like deep learning and reinforcement learning are pushing the boundaries of what is possible. For instance, neural networks can analyze even more complex relationships between variables, while reinforcement learning enables real-time price adjustments based on immediate feedback. These advancements herald a future where pricing strategies are not just data-driven but also autonomous and adaptive.

By harnessing the power of ML, businesses can stay ahead in a competitive landscape, offering prices that align with both market realities and customer expectations. Whether you are running a small business or a multinational enterprise, ML provides the tools to transform pricing from a reactive task into a forward-looking growth strategy.

Natural Language Processing (NLP): Understanding Customer Sentiment and Demand Drivers

Natural Language Processing (NLP) allows AI systems to comprehend and interpret human language, converting vast amounts of unstructured text into meaningful insights. From customer reviews to social media posts and support tickets, these data sources, often seen as disorganized, hold valuable information about how consumers perceive products, services, and pricing. By applying NLP, businesses can harness this data to better understand customer motivations, market trends, and the perceived value of their offerings.

In effect, NLP acts as a bridge between human expression and machine analysis. It decodes the subtleties of customer feedback and turns them into patterns that machines can evaluate. This capacity is particularly useful for pricing strategies, where grasping customer sentiment can determine the success or failure of an approach. For instance, NLP can assess whether customers view a product as "too expensive" or "offering great value" and can uncover shifts in sentiment around certain features or aspects of the pricing structure. These insights provide businesses with actionable intelligence on how to align pricing with consumer expectations (Joulin et al. 2017).

One main application of NLP in pricing is sentiment analysis. By evaluating customer feedback, NLP can quantify emotions and opinions about prices. For example, an online marketplace analyzed thousands of reviews with NLP and found that a sizable portion of their customers perceived their premium products as overpriced. With this knowledge, the company adjusted its pricing tiers to meet customer expectations, leading to a 20% improvement in satisfaction ratings (IBM 2023). This case illustrates how NLP can help businesses reveal pain points in their pricing strategies and address them by aligning more closely with customer sentiments.

NLP also plays a vital role in trend detection. By scanning social media, forums, and blogs, it can distinguish trends that could influence pricing decisions. For instance, NLP can analyze online discussions to reveal shifts in customer sentiment regarding product features. Liu et al. (2018) demonstrated how textual data analysis can generate actionable insights.

Consider a cosmetics brand that used NLP to analyze online conversations around a new product launch. The analysis revealed that consumers increasingly paying attention to eco-friendliness and sustainability. Armed with this knowledge, the company pivoted quickly to highlight the sustainable ingredients in its marketing narrative. Furthermore, recognizing that customers perceived eco-friendly products as premium, the company restructured its pricing strategy by introducing a tiered pricing model. For standard items, they kept existing prices, but for products featuring sustainable ingredients, they introduced a premium tier at a slightly higher price point. The transparent communication of the environmental benefits justified the price differential, leading to a 15% increase in sales. This case illustrates how NLP-powered trend analysis can directly impact pricing strategies, ensuring they remain aligned with shifting consumer values and market demands.

What makes NLP stand out is its ability to process and analyze enormous amounts of text quickly and efficiently. Traditional methods, such as surveys and focus groups, can only offer a static snapshot of customer sentiment, while NLP enables businesses to gain real-time insights from ongoing feedback. For instance, during a promotional event, a retailer monitored customer reactions to discounts using NLP. When negative feedback about a specific product category began circulating on social media, the retailer swiftly adjusted its promotion, avoiding potential customer dissatisfaction and improving overall campaign success (Chen et al. 2020).

These applications demonstrate how NLP can be a game changer in pricing, helping businesses understand customer behavior, react swiftly to market changes, and develop more targeted and effective pricing strategies.

Technical Insight

Implementing NLP tools does not require an advanced degree in computer science. Libraries like TextBlob and NLTK make it accessible for businesses of all sizes. Below is an example of performing sentiment analysis using Python's TextBlob library:

```
from textblob import TextBlob
import requests

# Fetch reviews from an API
api_url = 'https://api.example.com/reviews'  # Replace with your API endpoint
try:
    response = requests.get(api_url)
    if response.status_code == 200:
        reviews = response.json()  # Assuming the API returns a JSON array of reviews
    else:
        print(f"Failed to fetch reviews. Status code: {response.status_code}")
        reviews = []
except requests.exceptions.RequestException as e:
    print(f"An error occurred while fetching reviews: {e}")
    reviews = []

# Analyze sentiment for each review
if reviews:
    for review in reviews:
        sentiment = TextBlob(review).sentiment
        print(f"Review: {review}\nSentiment: {sentiment}")
else:
    print("No reviews available for analysis.")
```

This simple implementation shines a light on how businesses can effectively gauge sentiment. TextBlob assigns each review a polarity score, where positive scores reflect positive sentiment, and negative scores imply dissatisfaction. By scaling this analysis to thousands of reviews or posts, businesses can gain a holistic view of customer attitudes.

Looking Ahead

As NLP continues to advance, its applications in pricing are poised to grow even further. Emerging technologies like transformer-based models (e.g., BERT or GPT) enable more nuanced analysis, including context-aware sentiment detection and conversational understanding. Imagine an AI tool that not only spots dissatisfaction with pricing but also suggests alternative structures based on similar scenarios in the past. These developments are pushing the boundaries of how businesses can personalize pricing to better meet customer expectations.

With help of NLP, companies can do more than just react to customer feedback. In fact, they can anticipate needs, detect emerging trends, and make pricing decisions that feel intuitive and fair. In a world where customer sentiment increasingly drives purchasing decisions, NLP is a handy tool for staying competitive and connected to the people you serve.

Generative AI (Gen AI): Generating New Possibilities Based on Patterns in Data

Generative AI is expanding the boundaries of pricing strategies by offering innovative approaches to business challenges and opportunities. Unlike traditional AI, which typically analyzes existing data, Generative AI (Gen AI) has the unique ability to create new possibilities. It generates personalized pricing models, simulates various pricing scenarios, and even creates tailored promotional content that resonates with customers on an individual level. By combining historical data with contextual insights, Gen AI enables a level of precision and creativity in pricing that was previously unimaginable (Zhang and Xiong 2024).

One of the most powerful use cases of Generative AI lies in scenario simulation. For example, if a business is considering raising prices by 5% on its subscription service, Gen AI can model the potential outcomes, predicting how the price change could impact revenue and customer retention. With these projections in hand, businesses can make informed, data-driven decisions before implementing any changes. This predictive capability helps businesses navigate complex and fluctuating market conditions with confidence (Binns 2021).

Another compelling application of Gen AI is in dynamic content creation. Unlike traditional systems that analyze numerical data alone, Gen AI can communicate directly with customers through personalized messages. It can draft promotional materials, such as emails or SMS messages, which are tailored to customer behavior and preferences. For instance, an e-commerce business can use Gen AI to automatically send customized offers to customers who abandoned their shopping carts, increasing the likelihood of completing the purchase. These messages can dynamically adjust based on factors such as inventory levels, customer engagement history, or seasonal trends (Liu and Chen 2020).

A SaaS provider recently applied GPT-based Generative AI to simulate the effects of a 5% price hike. The model provided insights that balanced potential revenue increases with the risk of losing customers. As a result, the company implemented a tiered pricing strategy that maximized profits while minimizing customer churn (Built In 2023). This example illustrates how Gen AI does not just provide assistance but also actively informs and shapes pricing decisions with forward-thinking insights (Martinez and Liao 2021).

Furthermore, Generative AI is being used to design dynamic pricing experiments. A major e-commerce platform employed Gen AI to generate variations of discount strategies tailored to different customer segments. By analyzing the outcomes of these experiments, the company discovered the most effective strategy for driving conversions, achieving a 12% increase in sales during a promotional period (Zhang and Xiong 2024).

These applications underscore how Generative AI is revolutionizing pricing strategies, allowing businesses to move beyond traditional models and into more adaptive, personalized, and data-driven approaches.

Technical Insight

Generative AI platforms like Hugging Face's transformer models offer accessible ways to simulate pricing scenarios and generate creative content. Here is how you can use an open-source model, such as LLaMA 2, to simulate pricing scenarios:

```
from transformers import AutoModelForCausalLM, AutoTokenizer

# Load a newer model, e.g., LLaMA 2 or Falcon
model_name = "meta-llama/Llama-2-7b-chat-hf"  # Or "tiiuae/falcon-7b"
tokenizer = AutoTokenizer.from_pretrained(model_name)
model = AutoModelForCausalLM.from_pretrained(model_name)
```

```
# Generate pricing scenario
prompt = "What if subscription prices increase by 5%? Analyze
revenue and customer retention."
input_ids = tokenizer.encode(prompt, return_tensors="pt")
output = model.generate(input_ids, max_length=100)
print(tokenizer.decode(output[0], skip_special_tokens=True))
```

This example gives us an idea about how simple it can be to test pricing strategies using Gen AI. With slight modifications, businesses can explore countless "what-if" scenarios, refining their decisions without taking real-world risks.

Looking Ahead

As Generative AI evolves, its applications in pricing will proliferate further. For example, next-generation models can create highly localized pricing strategies by combining Gen AI with real-time market data. Picture a scenario where Gen AI instantly adjusts prices for a product in response to a competitor's discount or a sudden surge in demand. This capability could redefine agility in pricing strategies.

Furthermore, Gen AI's ability to craft tailored content could extend to real-time negotiation tools. Imagine equipping your sales team with an AI assistant that generates customer-specific pricing pitches during live conversations. By analyzing the customer's preferences, purchase history, and market conditions, the AI could suggest an optimal price point that aligns with both the company's goals and the customer's expectations.

Generative AI reimagines what is possible, as it empowers businesses to experiment, innovate, and communicate with unparalleled precision. As customer expectations evolve and markets grow more competitive, Gen AI provides the tools to stay ahead, ensuring pricing strategies are not only effective but also deeply aligned with customer need. In the world of AI-enabled pricing, Generative AI is the creative force that turns data into action and ideas into reality. Its ability to generate new possibilities ensures that businesses are prepared for the challenges today as well as the opportunities tomorrow.

Reinforcement Learning (RL): Adapting Prices in Real Time

Reinforcement Learning (RL) holds promise for enhancing pricing strategies, especially in fast-moving environments. Unlike traditional predictive models that rely on historical data, RL continuously interacts with its environment, learning from both successes and failures. It evolves by receiving feedback in the form of rewards and penalties, adjusting its strategy accordingly. For pricing applications, these rewards could represent increased revenue, while penalties might include issues like customer churn or unsold stock. The ability to adapt in real time makes RL especially valuable in industries where conditions change swiftly.

Consider a scenario where an airport is crowded with passengers on a stormy evening, flights are either delayed or canceled, and travelers scramble to find alternate flights. In this context, RL can help airlines adjust ticket prices dynamically, balancing available seats with fluctuating demand. Similarly, in the ride-hailing industry, RL helps set fares by considering factors like local traffic conditions, driver availability, and passenger demand, ensuring optimal pricing at any given time.

A powerful feature of RL is its application in dynamic pricing, where algorithms continuously adjust prices based on real-time factors such as demand, inventory levels, or competitor actions. For example, during a flash sale, an e-commerce site may use RL to adjust prices based on customer behavior, depending on whether a customer buys immediately or hesitates, enabling the platform to find the perfect balance between sales volume and profit margins.

RL's capabilities extend to sectors like airlines and ride-hailing services, where it can adapt prices based on constantly changing factors. For instance, an airline might employ RL to adjust ticket prices dynamically by analyzing booking trends, weather, and competitor pricing in real-time. This strategy led to a 12% increase in revenue per seat, showing RL's potential in competitive industries (Stanford HAI 2023). Similarly, ride-hailing apps, which often struggle with adjusting fares during peak times, utilize RL to adjust prices in real time. For example, during a snowstorm, RL can increase fares to reflect heightened demand without compromising affordability, benefiting both drivers and riders by optimizing earnings and ensuring service availability during critical periods. Rest assured that the ethical considerations in AI-enabled pricing will be discussed in greater detail in what follows.

Technical Insight

The mechanics of RL might sound complex, but they are rooted in a simple concept: learning through feedback. Below is a simplified example of a Q-learning algorithm, a foundational RL technique, applied to pricing:

```python
import numpy as np

# Define states and actions
states = ['low_demand', 'medium_demand', 'high_demand']
actions = ['low_price', 'medium_price', 'high_price']

# Initialize Q-table
q_table = np.zeros((len(states), len(actions)))

# Parameters
learning_rate = 0.1
discount_factor = 0.9
episodes = 1000

# Simulate environment
for episode in range(episodes):
    state = np.random.choice(len(states))
    action = np.random.choice(len(actions))
    reward = np.random.randint(-5, 20) #Simulated reward

    # Update Q-value
    next_state = np.random.choice(len(states))
    q_table[state, action] += learning_rate * (
        reward + discount_factor * np.max(q_table[next_
        state]) - q_table[state, action]
    )

print("Q-Table after training:")
print(q_table)
```

This code casts light on how RL learns to associate specific pricing actions with expected outcomes. Over time, the algorithm recognizes which pricing strategies yield the highest rewards in different demand scenarios.

Looking Ahead

The future of RL in pricing is exciting. Emerging RL techniques are being paired with deep learning to cope with more complex environments. For instance, airlines could use RL to optimize not only ticket prices but also ancillary services like baggage fees and meal upgrades. Similarly, subscription-based businesses might use RL to personalize pricing for individual customers, adjusting rates based on usage patterns and loyalty.

Another promising development is the integration of RL with multi-agent systems. Imagine a marketplace where RL algorithms for sellers and buyers interact, dynamically adjusting prices and negotiating deals in real time. This could revolutionize industries like wholesale, where pricing often involves complex negotiations.

Reinforcement Learning is conducive to continuous improvement. By learning from every interaction, RL empowers businesses to stay agile in the face of uncertainty. Whether it is optimizing ticket fares during peak travel times or dynamically pricing products during flash sales, RL ensures that businesses can adapt and thrive in real time.

In a world where customer expectations are constantly evolving, RL provides the flexibility and precision needed to deliver pricing strategies that are not only profitable but also fair and responsive. As businesses continue to embrace this technology, RL is set to play a pivotal role in shaping the future of AI-enabled pricing.

Explainable AI (XAI): Building Trust in Pricing Decisions

Explainable AI (XAI) addresses one of the biggest hurdles in AI adoption: trust. As businesses increasingly turn to AI for pricing decisions, stakeholders, employees, and customers may feel uncertainty about how these decisions are made. For example, why would the AI recommend raising the price of one product while offering a discount on another? How do these decisions align with organizational goals, legal standards, or customer expectations? XAI alleviates these concerns by offering clear, comprehensible explanations about how AI models operate and why they arrive at specific pricing recommendations.

In the world of pricing, transparency is crucial. AI systems are often seen as "black boxes"—complex entities that generate results without revealing the underlying process (Yang 2024). This lack of clarity can lead to hesitation among decision-makers and frustration among customers. XAI creates transparency by breaking down pricing decisions into logical, traceable steps, making them easier for stakeholders to understand and trust. This clarity is not just a luxury for pricing teams; it is necessary for regulatory compliance, customer satisfaction, and organizational alignment.

One important use case of XAI in pricing is ensuring adherence to regulations. Pricing decisions in industries such as insurance or telecommunications often face scrutiny for fairness and legality. XAI tools help businesses ensure that their pricing models are in line with regulatory requirements by providing explanations for every decision made by the system. For instance, an insurance company using AI for policy pricing can use XAI to verify that the algorithm does not discriminate based on sensitive factors. This ability to convey transparency can help minimize the risk of legal challenges.

XAI also plays a significant part in fostering customer trust. Imagine a subscription service that increases its prices. Without an explanation, customers might perceive the change as arbitrary or unfair, which could lead to backlash or even cancellations. However, by using XAI to clearly communicate the reasons behind the price adjustment such as cost increases due to inflation or added features, customers are more likely to understand and accept the change. Transparent and well-explained pricing decisions promote fairness, turning potential conflicts into opportunities for stronger customer relationships.

For example, a retailer implemented XAI to facilitate AI-enabled price adjustments. The system assessed factors such as historical sales data, competitor pricing, and demand forecasts to recommend new prices. Before acting on these suggestions, the retailer employed XAI to review the rationale behind each price change to ensure it aligned with the brand's core values and customer expectations. This kind of transparency not only improved internal decision-making but also strengthened customer trust, as the retailer could provide clear explanations about the rationale behind their price adjustments (Devabit 2023).

Technical Insight

XAI can be deployed with help of robust tools like SHAP (SHapley Additive exPlanations), which provide detailed insights into AI model predictions. Below is an example of how SHAP can be used to explain pricing recommendations:

```
import shap
from sklearn.ensemble import RandomForestRegressor
from sklearn.model_selection import train_test_split
import pandas as pd

# Load data
data = pd.read_csv("pricing_data.csv")
X = data[['demand', 'competitor_price', 'cost']]
y = data['optimal_price']
```

```
# Train model
model = RandomForestRegressor()
X_train, X_test, y_train, y_test = train_test_split(X, y,
test_size=0.2, random_state=42)
model.fit(X_train, y_train)

# Explain predictions
explainer = shap.Explainer(model, X_train)
shap_values = explainer(X_test)

# Visualize explanation for a single prediction
shap.plots.waterfall(shap_values[0])
```

This code gives us a clue about how SHAP assigns importance to each feature in a model's prediction. For example, it might show that a competitor's price heavily influenced the AI's recommendation for a particular product. These insights would allow pricing teams to validate decisions and adjust strategies as needed.

Looking Ahead

The role of XAI in pricing is evolving rapidly. One exciting application is real-time explainability, where AI systems provide justifications as they generate recommendations. For instance, a dynamic pricing tool might explain, in real time, that it is raising the price of a product due to high demand during a promotional event. Another emerging application is visual storytelling, where XAI uses graphs, charts, and narratives to communicate complex decisions in an intuitive way.

Additionally, XAI is becoming steadily more user-friendly. Tools like LIME (Local Interpretable Model-agnostic Explanations) and integrated XAI dashboards are making it easier for non-technical stakeholders to interact with and understand AI systems. This democratization of AI transparency ensures that everyone, from data scientists to frontline managers, can contribute to smarter pricing decisions.

By shedding light on the reasoning behind AI recommendations, XAI enables companies to align their strategies with regulatory standards, organizational goals, and customer expectations. This transparency creates a virtuous cycle: clearer decisions lead to greater trust, which, in turn, drives more confident adoption of AI in pricing.

In an era where customers expect both value and fairness, XAI could provide a distinct competitive edge. Businesses that embrace transparency will not only make better pricing decisions but also build lasting relationships with stakeholders and customers alike. As pricing strategies grow more sophisticated, XAI ensures that the human element stays at the heart of every decision.

Synthetic Data Generation: Overcoming Data Gaps

Synthetic data is reshaping how companies approach pricing by enabling them to create artificial datasets that closely mirror real-world data. This innovation is a practical alternative to relying on sensitive, incomplete, or difficult-to-access information. By using synthetic data, businesses can ensure privacy and security while still being able to train AI models and derive actionable insights, even in situations where actual data is scarce or hard to obtain.

One of the most notable advantages of synthetic data is its ability to simulate hypothetical market conditions. For instance, companies can generate data to understand how demand might fluctuate under various pricing strategies, such as during economic downturns or amidst supply chain disruptions. These simulations allow businesses to explore various "what-if" scenarios without the risk of using actual data or prematurely making potentially damaging decisions.

Synthetic data plays an important role in safeguarding privacy as well. In sectors like healthcare, finance, or retail, where handling customer data comes with significant regulatory constraints, using real customer data for training AI models may pose compliance challenges. By generating synthetic data that replicates customer behaviors while removing personal identifiers, businesses can continue to work with AI effectively while ensuring they follow privacy regulations such as GDPR or CCPA. This capability helps businesses uphold ethical standards while making data-driven decisions.

A global retailer, for example, faced significant pricing challenges due to supply chain disruptions, fluctuating demand, and unpredictable raw material availability. Rather than relying on incomplete or sensitive data, they utilized synthetic data to simulate market conditions, enabling them to test different pricing strategies, adjust in real time, and refine their approach, all while safeguarding customer privacy (IBM 2023).

The use of synthetic data in this instance allowed the retailer to make more informed decisions without risking exposure of real data to security vulnerabilities or regulatory non-compliance. Additionally, it provided them with a flexibility that traditional data collection methods could not match, allowing them to quickly adapt to rapidly changing market conditions.

Technical Insight

Generating synthetic data is more accessible than ever, thanks to libraries like NumPy and Pandas in Python. These tools allow businesses to create datasets that reflect the key variables influencing pricing decisions, such as demand fluctuations, competitor prices, and cost structures. Below is an example of how synthetic data can be generated to simulate a pricing environment:

```
import numpy as np
import pandas as pd

# Generate synthetic data
np.random.seed(42)
synthetic_data = {
    "demand": np.random.randint(100, 500, 100),
    "competitor_price": np.random.uniform(20, 50, 100),
    "cost": np.random.uniform(10, 30, 100),
    "optimal_price": np.random.uniform(25, 55, 100)
}

# Create DataFrame
synthetic_df = pd.DataFrame(synthetic_data)
print(synthetic_df.head())
```

This code creates a dataset of 100 entries, including variables like demand, competitor price, cost, and the optimal price subject to the company's goal hierarchy. The generated dataset mimics the type of information a business might use to assess different pricing strategies. By generating synthetic data this way, businesses can conduct model training and scenario analysis without needing to rely on real customer information, making it easier to iterate and refine their pricing approaches.

Looking Ahead

Future developments may allow for even more sophisticated data generation techniques, where synthetic data not only mimics real-world behavior but also accounts for complex, non-linear relationships between variables. For instance, as businesses embrace AI-powered dynamic pricing, synthetic data will play a major part in training algorithms to adapt to micro-trends and unpredictable market shifts.

Another exciting development is the combination of synthetic data with reinforcement learning (RL). By generating simulated pricing environments, businesses can train RL models that adapt and evolve their pricing strategies based on hypothetical feedback without having to wait for real-world market changes. This combination of technologies could lead to even more agile, responsive, and personalized pricing systems.

Synthetic data is not just a temporary workaround for incomplete datasets; it is a powerful tool that enables businesses to innovate and experiment with pricing strategies in a risk-free, ethical, and scalable way. That being said, its effectiveness depends on how well it can replicate the complexities and nuances of real human data, which remains an area of active research and potential limitation. As the regulatory landscape around data privacy tightens and the need for agility in pricing increases, synthetic data offers a promising resource for companies aiming to stay competitive in the data-driven age. By allowing businesses to harness the power of AI without compromising privacy, it has the potential to support more ethical and dynamic pricing practices while continuing to evolve in its fidelity to real-world scenarios.

Conclusion

AI technologies are powerful forces reshaping how businesses approach pricing. By incorporating machine learning (ML) for predictive analytics, natural language processing (NLP) for customer sentiment analysis, generative AI (Gen AI) for simulating pricing scenarios, reinforcement learning (RL) for real-time price adjustments, explainable AI (XAI) for building trust, and synthetic data generation for robust model training, companies can craft pricing strategies that are more intelligent, flexible, and customer-focused.

The synergy between these technologies is electrifying. When combined, they form a pricing framework that is not only proactive and adaptable but also transparent and responsive to shifts in market conditions and customer needs. As companies continue to integrate these AI tools, the future of pricing will no longer be limited to simple optimization but will focus on redefining value in ways that foster mutual benefit for both businesses and their customers.

AI-Enabled Pricing Process

Implementing AI in pricing is akin to crafting a masterpiece. It begins with raw data, which is shaped and refined using AI models before being scaled and rolled out across the organization. Throughout this journey, there will be hurdles, moments of uncertainty and setbacks, and eventually breakthroughs that refine your pricing strategy into something far more impactful than initially envisioned. This is a process that demands patience, flexibility, and, most importantly, a clear understanding of both your business goals and the tools available.

Consider this endeavor as navigating a constantly changing landscape. While the tools at your disposal are advanced, the path is often unclear. You start with data, raw and potentially incomplete, yet critical to the process. That data is then fed into AI models, which are adjusted to respond to the realities of the market. However, the true transformation comes about when these models are deployed at scale, influencing real-time pricing decisions, and becoming integrated into the entire organization.

While the technical intricacies may be overwhelming at times, the steps of implementing AI in pricing are relatively straightforward. Initially, the data must be cleaned and structured to ensure it is relevant and actionable. Once this is done, the appropriate AI models must be selected and trained to ensure the results align with business objectives. Then there is this challenge in scaling the solution across the organization. This is where the magic truly happens. When AI is no longer just a concept but a fully realized system influencing decisions and driving business results, the potential is unlocked.

This section will delve into each phase of AI implementation, highlighting the key challenges and strategies involved. By the end, you will not only understand how AI functions but also how to use it to revolutionize your pricing strategy. Whether you are starting from nothing or optimizing an existing system, mastering these phases is essential for maximizing the benefits of AI in pricing.

Phase 1: Data Preparation and Cleaning—The Engine Behind AI Success

When people think about AI, they are inclined to focus on the sophisticated algorithms and the speed with which they can generate insights, such as predicting customer behavior, optimizing pricing, or personalizing recommendations. These impressive AI applications often steal the spotlight. However, behind every success lies the less glamorous yet equally essential process of data preparation. Think of it as cleaning the kitchen before preparing a meal. It may not be exciting, but it is absolutely critical to ensure everything runs smoothly.

Picture this: You are getting ready to cook your favorite dish, but the kitchen is chaotic. Dirty dishes, a messy fridge, and a cluttered counter. Trying to cook in that environment would be difficult and frustrating at best, if not entirely unfeasible. The same holds true for AI. If the data fed into your models is incomplete, inconsistent, or poorly organized, the outputs will be equally flawed. The algorithm can only work with what it is given, so poor-quality data results in poor-quality predictions.

There is this mid-sized retailer, who faced this challenge firsthand. Eager to tap the potential of AI, they jumped into training complex models with the expectation that the system would quickly yield valuable insights. However, the predictions were inconsistent and unreliable. Some models suggested prices that were too low, while others recommended prices that customers would never accept. After much frustration, they realized the issue was not the AI; it was the data. The dataset had missing entries, duplicate records, and outdated customer information. What seemed like a quick win turned into months of rework.

Determined to resolve the issue, the retailer took a step back and started over with the basics. They combined data from their CRM and sales platforms, cleaned the dataset, and standardized the formats. After addressing the duplicates and ensuring accuracy, they retrained the AI models. This time, the results were consistent and dependable, yielding actionable insights that enhanced their pricing strategy and boosted revenue.

No matter how advanced your AI system is, poor-quality data will always lead to poor outcomes. The accuracy of your results is directly tied to the quality of the data you input. Therefore, before deploying AI-powered pricing models, investing time and resources in data preparation is critical. It is the foundational step that ensures the entire AI initiative succeeds.

In fact, research suggests that up to 80% of the time spent on an AI project can be attributed to data preparation (Loukides 2020a, b). No matter how sophisticated the AI models, they are only as effective as the data they have been trained on. Cleaning, consolidating, and structuring the data is not just a technical task. It is a strategic one that sets the stage for AI to deliver its full potential. Now, let's dive into the key steps involved in preparing data for AI applications.

1. Identifying and Collecting Relevant Data

The initial step in preparing data for AI is deciding which data will be most valuable for achieving the specific goal at hand. In the context of pricing, this involves gathering the right mix of data to guide effective decisions. As discussed previously, key categories of relevant data for AI-enabled pricing strategies typically include:

- **Transactional Data**: This type includes historical sales data, customer behaviors, product details, and pricing information. It helps businesses understand past market dynamics, identify trends, and model future demand (Davenport and Bean 2020).
- **Customer Behavior Data**: Demographic details, browsing history, and past purchase behaviors offer insights into customer preferences and price sensitivity, helping to craft more personalized pricing models (Choudhury et al. 2022).
- **Market Trend Data**: Information on competitor pricing, external factors such as seasonality, economic trends, and global events can influence pricing decisions, helping businesses anticipate shifts in demand or supply (Brynjolfsson and McAfee 2017).

After deciding on relevant data sources, the next challenge is to collect and organize this information into a centralized repository. Organizations often face difficulties with fragmented data scattered across multiple systems, such as CRM platforms, ERP systems, and spreadsheets. To overcome this, integrating these disparate data sources into a unified system is crucial. Solutions like **Snowflake** and **Amazon Web Services (AWS)** proved effective in merging data, providing businesses with seamless access to a comprehensive dataset (Chen et al. 2021). By centralizing the data, companies ensure that AI models receive accurate, consistent information, enabling them to make more informed and effective pricing decisions.

In summary, proper data identification and consolidation are fundamental steps for AI-enabled pricing to achieve its full potential. Organizations that streamline this process are well-poised to utilize AI's predictive and adaptive capabilities effectively.

2. Cleaning the Data: The Essential Foundation

Cleaning data is one of the most resource-intensive and crucial steps in data preparation for AI implementation. Without clean, accurate data, even the most advanced AI models can yield flawed results, jeopardizing pricing decisions. This process involves a few steps designed to address errors, inconsistencies, and gaps that could undermine the effectiveness of AI-enabled pricing models.

A. Handling Missing Data

Missing data is a common issue, appearing as blank cells, rows, or columns in datasets. For example, in a customer transaction database, missing entries in fields like "purchase amount" can lead to incomplete analyses.

- **Imputation**: One approach to address missing values is imputation, where values are replaced with statistical estimates like the mean, median, or mode. For example, if 10% of a "discount percentage" column is missing, filling those gaps with the column's average value may provide continuity. More sophisticated methods, like regression models or machine learning-based imputations, can also estimate missing values more accurately (Little and Rubin 2020).
- **Deletion**: When missing data is too extensive or would distort analysis, rows or columns with incomplete entries can be removed. However, this should be done sparingly to avoid discarding valuable information. Sparse columns with negligible significance might be dropped to streamline the dataset.

B. Eliminating Duplicate Records

Duplicate entries often arise from multiple data imports, system glitches, or user input errors. Left unchecked, they can inflate transaction volumes or misrepresent customer behavior, skewing AI model results. Programming tools like Python's Pandas library offer efficient ways to detect and drop duplicate entries. A simple command such as df.drop_duplicates() can streamline this process, ensuring each record appears only once.

C. Standardizing Data

Inconsistent formatting in datasets can create significant challenges for AI models. Discrepancies such as varying date formats like "DD-MM-YYYY" in one section and "YYYY-MM-DD" in another or mixed capitalization in text fields must be resolved to ensure consistency.

- **Date Format Consistency:** Standardizing date formats ensures accurate temporal analyses. Libraries like Pandas provide methods like pd.to_datetime() to convert dates into uniform formats.

- **Text Standardization**: Text fields, especially those capturing qualitative feedback, should be normalized. Converting all entries to lowercase, for instance, ensures consistent categorization and comparison, particularly when analyzing customer sentiment or product feedback.

D. Identifying and Correcting Outliers

Outliers, i.e., extreme values that deviate significantly from the rest of the dataset, can distort AI-enabled predictions. For example, a data entry erroneously listing a product price as $999,999 instead of $99.99 could mislead algorithms into generating unrealistic recommendations.

Detection Methods:

Visualization tools like box plots or statistical approaches such as Z-scores and the Interquartile Range (IQR) method are effective for spotting anomalies.

Remediation Strategies:

Outliers may either be corrected, excluded, or reanalyzed based on their context. Erroneous entries can be replaced with realistic estimates, while legitimate but unusual data points may be retained if they contribute critical insights.

E. Data Transformation and Normalization

Data transformation and normalization are fundamental steps in readying datasets for AI applications, ensuring that all features contribute equitably to the model's learning process. In real-world datasets, variables often have vastly different ranges and units. This disparity can cause certain features to dominate the model's calculations, leading to skewed predictions. For instance, in a pricing model, sales revenue might span from $1 to $10,000, while competitor prices may range from $10 to $500. Without adjusting for these differences, the model might disproportionately emphasize the feature with the broader range (i.e., sales revenue), resulting in biased outcomes.

To address these disparities, data transformation techniques scale all features to comparable ranges or units of measurement, ensuring that the model assigns them equal importance. Two widely used methods for achieving this balance are **Min-Max Scaling** and **Z-score Normalization**.

1. Min-Max Scaling: Min-Max Scaling adjusts the range of a feature to fall within a predefined interval, typically [0,1]. This technique ensures that all values align consistently, improving the model's efficiency during training. It is especially useful for features like prices, ratings, or quantities that need to be represented within a uniform range.

The formula for Min-Max Scaling is:

$$X' = \frac{X - \min(X)}{\max(X) - \min(X)}$$

where X' is the scaled value, X is the original value, $\min(X)$ is the minimum value, and $\max(X)$ is the maximum value of the feature. This transformation is particularly useful when you need a consistent range for features like prices, ratings, or quantities. For instance, a retailer analyzing product pricing might use Min-Max Scaling to bring all price values into a [0,1] range, ensuring consistency in comparisons and accelerating model convergence.

2. **Z-score Normalization (Standardization):** Z-score normalization transforms data by centering it around a mean of 0 and scaling it to a standard deviation of 1. This approach is ideal when features have varying variances or when the data follows a normal distribution, as it ensures that all variables are treated equally, regardless of their original scales.

The formula for Z-score Normalization is:

$$X' = \frac{X - \mu}{\sigma}$$

where X' is the normalized value, X is the original value, μ is the mean of the feature, and σ is the standard deviation. This method is particularly effective for features prone to outliers, such as customer income or transaction frequency, as it reduces the impact of extreme values.

Scaling and normalizing data are critical steps in preparing datasets for AI models, as they ensure that no single feature disproportionately influences the learning process due to its scale or variance. By transforming data into a consistent format, AI models can better identify patterns and relationships across variables, rather than being skewed by disparate scales. This approach significantly enhances the precision of models used for pricing optimization, customer segmentation, and demand forecasting, ensuring that all relevant features are weighted fairly.

The choice between Min-Max Scaling and Z-score Normalization depends on the dataset's characteristics and the problem at hand. Min-Max Scaling is particularly effective when features need to be constrained within a specific range, such as [0,1], making it ideal for datasets involving bounded quantities like percentages or ratings. On the other hand, Z-score Normalization is better suited for datasets with diverse units or where outliers might distort results, as it standardizes values by centering them around a mean of zero and scaling to a standard deviation of one. Both techniques provide a structured approach to handling data variability, enabling AI systems to produce more accurate and reliable outcomes.

3. Feature Engineering: Refining the Dataset

Feature engineering stands out as one of the most impactful and innovative steps in preparing data for AI models. This process involves transforming raw datasets into new, insightful features that enhance the model's ability to recognize patterns and relationships within the data. Think of it as sculpting a block of marble into a finely detailed statue. When done effectively, feature engineering can uncover hidden insights that dramatically improve the predictive power of AI models.

In the context of pricing models, feature engineering is instrumental in creating variables that may not be immediately obvious but are pivotal for predicting outcomes and optimizing strategies. By carefully crafting features that align with specific business objectives, you enable AI systems to deliver sharper predictions and provide actionable insights, fostering more informed and strategic pricing decisions.

A. Developing New Features

A vital aspect of feature engineering involves creating new variables from existing data to highlight patterns and insights relevant to your pricing model. This process often includes aggregating raw data into more meaningful metrics that reflect customer behavior or product performance. By crafting these new features, businesses can derive deeper insights to inform pricing strategies.

For example, transactional data alone may not directly reveal trends in customer loyalty, profitability, or purchasing patterns. However, transforming this raw data into engineered features can unlock valuable information that drives more informed decision-making.

- **Average Purchase Value per Customer**: Calculating the average amount spent by each customer over a specified time frame can provide insights into their typical spending behavior. High-value customers, for example, may be less sensitive to price changes, making them more likely to tolerate price increases. Conversely, customers with lower average spending levels might react negatively to even slight price hikes.

- **Customer Lifetime Value (CLV)**: CLV combines historical purchase data with predictive metrics to estimate the total revenue a customer will generate throughout their relationship with your company. This feature is particularly useful for uncovering high-value customers and tailoring pricing strategies to maximize their lifetime value. For example, businesses may offer personalized discounts or promotions to encourage loyalty from these profitable segments.
- **Price Elasticity**: Measuring how demand fluctuates with changes in price, price elasticity provides a way to gauge customer sensitivity. For instance, customers who continue purchasing a product after a price increase manifest lower elasticity, suggesting that they are less price-sensitive. Conversely, those who quickly reduce their purchases in response to a price hike are more price-sensitive. By calculating elasticity across various customer segments, businesses can adjust pricing dynamically to balance revenue generation with customer retention.

These engineered features significantly enhance the effectiveness of AI models by incorporating insights into customer behavior and market responsiveness. By embracing such data transformations, businesses can fine-tune their pricing strategies for maximum impact.

B. Encoding Categorical Data: Making Non-Numeric Information Usable

It is common to come across datasets with categorical variables, such as "region," "customer segment," or "product type." While this data is crucial for understanding trends and behaviors, it is not immediately suitable for machine learning models, which typically require numerical input. Categorical encoding bridges this gap by converting non-numeric categories into numerical values that AI algorithms can effectively process.

- **One-Hot Encoding**: One of the most widely used techniques, one-hot encoding transforms each unique category into a binary (0 or 1) variable. For example, if the "region" column in your dataset includes categories like "North," "South," and "East," this method will generate three separate columns: one for each region. If a particular transaction belongs to the "North" region, the "North" column will be marked as 1, while the others remain 0.

This method avoids implying any hierarchy or magnitude among the categories, which could occur if they were represented with integers (e.g., assigning 1 to "North," 2 to "South," etc.). Such misrepresentation might skew the model's learning process and affect its predictions.

- **Label Encoding**: Another approach is label encoding, where each category is assigned an integer value. For instance, if you have a "service level" column with values like "low," "medium," and "high," label encoding could assign these as 1, 2, and 3, respectively. This technique works well when the categories have an inherent order or ranking. For example, in this case, the model would understand that "high" priority holds more significance than "medium" or "low," in line with the nature of the data.

Both one-hot encoding and label encoding serve critical roles in converting categorical data into machine-readable formats. The choice of method depends on the characteristics of the dataset and the relationships among the categories. One-hot encoding is generally preferred for nominal data (categories with no inherent order), while label encoding is more suitable for ordinal data (categories with a clear hierarchy).

These transformations ensure that categorical data is accurately represented and integrated into machine learning workflows, enabling AI models to process and use this information effectively in pricing strategies and beyond.

C. Aggregating Data: Uncovering Trends Across Time and Customer Segments

Data aggregation is another fundamental process in feature engineering, particularly in pricing models, where key insights often surface only when examining trends over time or across specific customer groups. Aggregating data involves summarizing raw, granular information into a higher-level overview such as by week, month, or customer segment, enabling businesses to identify patterns and trends that are less apparent in detailed transactional datasets.

- **Temporal Aggregation**: Summarizing data over defined time periods, such as daily, weekly, or monthly, sheds light on seasonal trends, fluctuations, or demand shifts that influence pricing strategies. For instance, a retailer might aggregate daily sales data to the monthly level to reveal that certain winter products consistently sell better in December. Armed with this knowledge, the retailer can strategically increase prices during high-demand periods, optimizing profitability while aligning with seasonal demand patterns.

- **Customer Segment Aggregation**: By grouping data according to customer demographics or behavioral attributes such as "loyal customers" or "occasional buyers," businesses can uncover purchasing habits unique to specific groups. For example, aggregating data for high-value customers may reveal that they are less sensitive to incremental price increases compared to price-sensitive segments. This insight enables businesses to fine-tune pricing, offer personalized discounts, or sustain premium pricing for different segments, thereby maximizing revenue without alienating key customer groups.

Aggregating data provides a higher-level perspective, allowing AI models to recognize trends and behavioral patterns that might remain hidden in raw, transaction-level data. This broader view empowers businesses to dynamically adjust pricing strategies based on both long-term historical trends and real-time shifts in customer behavior. In doing so, aggregation becomes a cornerstone of effective data-driven decision-making in AI-powered pricing systems.

D. Key Takeaways

Feature engineering is an essential step for enhancing the performance and precision of AI models. By deriving meaningful features from raw datasets, you equip the model with relevant and insightful information, enabling it to generate more accurate predictions and actionable decisions. In pricing, this process allows for strategies that not only incorporate historical trends but also adapt to customer preferences, competitor movements, and external variables such as seasonality.

In addition, feature engineering aids the development of refined, customer-focused pricing frameworks. Instead of resorting to broad and generic pricing methods, businesses can segment customers and customize prices to align with individual behaviors and needs. This level of personalization enhances both profitability and customer satisfaction, making feature engineering a vital investment in the data preparation process.

The true potential of AI-enabled pricing often manifests itself during the feature engineering phase. By transforming raw datasets into targeted insights, businesses train AI models to better comprehend relationships and patterns in the data. Whether you are creating features to highlight customer lifetime value, encoding categorical variables for improved processing, or aggregating data to identify trends over time, these efforts lay the groundwork for smarter and more adaptable pricing strategies. Effective feature engineering drives informed decision-making, fostering success in competitive, dynamic markets.

4. Splitting Data for Training and Testing

Once your dataset is cleaned and enriched, the next step is splitting it into training and testing subsets. This process ensures that your AI model can learn effectively while also being evaluated on unseen data to measure its real-world performance. Think of it as preparing for an exam: you study using familiar materials (training data) but demonstrate your understanding by answering new questions (testing data).

Typically, a dataset is divided with 80% allocated for training and 20% for testing. The training data helps the model uncover patterns, relationships, and trends, while the testing data assesses how well the model generalizes to data it has not encountered before. This distinction is vital to avoid overfitting, a scenario where the model performs exceptionally well on training data but fails to adapt to new, unseen cases.

Consider a retailer employing AI to forecast demand for a particular product. If the model's accuracy is tested only on the same data used for training, it may appear flawless. However, such results do not provide a realistic gauge of its performance in future predictions. By using a separate testing subset, the retailer ensures the AI system can adapt to real-world conditions, offering reliable and actionable insights for future decision-making.

This step not only confirms the robustness of the model but also builds confidence that the AI is capable of handling dynamic, real-world scenarios with consistency and accuracy.

A. Splitting Data: Initializing the Datasets

Random Sampling

Random sampling is the most widely used method for dividing data into training and testing subsets. This method ensures that both subsets are representative of the overall dataset, minimizing the risk of skewed results. However, proper management of the randomness is crucial to avoid imbalances, such as one subset disproportionately representing a specific product category or time period.

Example: Imagine a subscription-based service aiming to predict customer churn. If the testing dataset happens to include mostly long-term subscribers, while the training data predominantly focuses on newer customers, the model might fail to generalize effectively. By using random sampling, both datasets can include a balanced mix of customer types, improving the model's performance and reliability.

Stratified Sampling

For datasets with imbalanced classes, such as when a minority of customers churn while the majority do not, stratified sampling should be considered as an effective alternative. This technique ensures that both the training and testing subsets keep the same proportional class distribution as the original dataset. This approach is especially critical in pricing models, where different customer segments like premium vs. standard-tier users might exhibit significantly varied behaviors.

Example: A SaaS company forecasting churn for premium and standard-tier customers might face challenges if one dataset disproportionately represents a specific customer group. By applying stratified sampling, the training and testing sets retain the actual distribution of these customer tiers, preventing the model from producing biased predictions.

Stratified sampling is particularly advantageous when working with imbalanced data, as it allows AI models to capture the nuances of each class more effectively while ensuring predictions remain equitable and accurate. This is essential for building robust and fair pricing strategies that cater to diverse customer segments.

B. Cross-Validation: Elevating Model Evaluation

To achieve a more thorough and reliable evaluation of an AI model's performance, K-fold cross-validation is a valuable technique. Unlike traditional data splitting methods, which create a single training and testing set, K-fold cross-validation divides the dataset into K equal subsets or "folds." The model is trained on K-1 folds while the remaining fold serves as the testing set. This process is repeated K times, with each fold used as the testing set once, ensuring every data point contributes to both training and evaluation.

Cross-validation enhances the robustness of model performance metrics by reducing the impact of a potentially unrepresentative data split. By applying this method, businesses can evaluate models comprehensively, ensuring they generalize well to unseen data and perform reliably across different scenarios.

Example: Consider a pricing model for airline tickets. The dataset encompasses diverse conditions such as peak travel seasons, off-peak periods, and last-minute bookings. K-fold cross-validation ensures the model performs properly on each of these conditions, delivering a pricing strategy that adapts effectively to a wide range of real-world situations.

How It Works? Let's assume a dataset with 1000 entries and set K to 5:

- The dataset is divided into five equal subsets, each containing 200 entries.
- The model is trained on 800 entries and tested on the remaining 200.
- This process is repeated five times, with a different fold serving as the testing set during each iteration.

The final performance metric is calculated by averaging the results from all five folds, offering a more reliable evaluation compared to a single split.

Technical Insight

In Python, this method can be implemented using libraries like scikit-learn, which offers convenient tools for cross-validation. Below is an example:

```python
from sklearn.model_selection import KFold, cross_val_score
from sklearn.ensemble import RandomForestRegressor

# Sample dataset and model
X = dataset.drop('target', axis=1)
y = dataset['target']
model = RandomForestRegressor()

# K-Fold Cross-Validation
kf = KFold(n_splits=5, shuffle=True, random_state=42)
cv_scores = cross_val_score(model, X, y, cv=kf)

print("Average CV Score:", cv_scores.mean())
```

This technique ensures that model evaluation accounts for the full variability within the data, providing a balanced and dependable assessment of how the AI system will perform in real-world applications.

Dividing data into training and testing sets may seem like a straightforward task, but it is also a crucial step in creating reliable AI-enabled pricing models. This process ensures that the model not only excels at analyzing historical data but also performs accurately when faced with new, unseen scenarios. By employing methods like random sampling, stratified sampling, and cross-validation, businesses can build pricing systems that are dependable, adaptable, and scalable. These techniques provide the groundwork for strategies that maximize impact while minimizing errors, setting the stage for long-term success in dynamic market environments.

Phase 2: Model Selection and Training—Choosing the Right Approach

Once your data is clean, enriched, and divided into training and testing sets, the next significant task is selecting the most appropriate AI model. Think of this step like choosing the right tool for a DIY project: a hammer is ideal for driving nails, but it would be awkward for cutting wood. Similarly, different AI models are built for specific purposes and selecting the wrong one can lead to inefficiency or inaccurate results.

The good news is that the wide variety of AI models available and you are likely to find one that best suits your particular pricing challenge. For instance, if your goal is to predict the optimal price for a product, regression models might be the best fit. On the other hand, if you aim to categorize customers into groups such as "bargain hunters" or "premium buyers," classification or clustering models would be more suitable. The key is to thoroughly understand your business objectives and match them with the strengths of each model, ensuring that the chosen AI tool effectively addresses your specific pricing needs.

By carefully assessing capabilities of different AI models with regard to your business goals, you can better ensure the accuracy and effectiveness of your pricing strategies. This thoughtful selection process sets the foundation for building robust AI-enabled pricing systems that not only analyze past data but also adapt to future market conditions with precision and confidence.

1. Selecting the Right Models

Before diving into specific AI models, let's take a moment to untangle two related but distinct ideas: AI technologies and AI models. Think of AI technologies like Machine Learning (ML), Natural Language Processing (NLP), and Reinforcement Learning (RL) as the big-picture frameworks or toolkits that make AI work. They provide the foundation, the capabilities, and the overarching methodologies for tackling complex problems.

AI models, on the other hand, are the specialized tools built within these technologies to solve specific tasks. If AI technologies are the toolkits, models are the wrenches, screwdrivers, and hammers you pull out for a particular job. While the technologies define the broad approach, the models zero in on executing it in a precise, tailored way.

For example, ML is an AI technology focused on training systems to identify patterns and make predictions. Within ML, there are models like regression for forecasting continuous outcomes, such as predicting price trends, and classification models for categorizing data, like sorting customers into distinct groups. NLP, as a technology, focuses on understanding and generating human language. Its models, such as transformers, help businesses analyze customer sentiment or detect shifts in demand. Similarly, RL, a technology designed for decision-making in dynamic environments, uses algorithms to refine strategies over time, learning through trial and error.

Imagine applying these concepts to pricing strategies. If you want to predict future price trends, you might use a regression model within the ML technology. To cluster customers based on their buying habits, you would make use of clustering models like k-means. For tasks like analyzing customer feedback or sentiment, NLP models such as BERT or GPT can transform unstructured text into actionable insights. If your pricing strategy requires adapting to real-time changes, like in ride-sharing or airline ticket pricing, RL algorithms would be your go-to choice, learning and optimizing decisions as conditions evolve.

The key is understanding that technologies set the stage, providing the broad capabilities, while models get into the nitty-gritty details, solving the specific challenges that you want to tackle. By grasping the distinction between AI technologies and AI models, you will be able to pick the right tools for achieving your goals. Whether forecasting prices, segmenting customers, or optimizing decisions in real time, knowing which model to use within the right technology ensures that you can benefit from the full potential of AI in formulating your pricing strategies.

A. Regression Models: Predicting Continuous Outcomes

Regression models are powerful tools in pricing analytics, ideal for forecasting continuous variables such as optimal prices, demand patterns, or projected revenues. These models construct mathematical relationships between dependent variables (e.g., sales revenue) and independent variables (e.g., production costs, competitor pricing), uncovering actionable trends that support data-driven decision-making.

For instance, a fashion retailer used multiple linear regression to set prices for a new seasonal clothing line. By analyzing factors like production costs, historical sales, competitor rates, and seasonal trends, the model highlighted opportunities to increase prices on premium items while keeping competitive rates for entry-level products. This targeted approach improved seasonal revenue by 12% within a single quarter.

Regression models are usually straightforward to interpret and highly effective in pricing scenarios involving continuous data. They are especially valuable for predicting future trends or assessing the impact of external factors like marketing campaigns on sales performance.

B. Classification Models: Categorizing for Strategic Decisions

Classification models are designed to sort data into predefined categories, making them indispensable for answering questions such as "Will this customer respond positively to a price change?" or "Which customer segment is most likely to redeem a discount offer?" These models help businesses make informed decisions at scale.

For example, a fitness subscription app employed logistic regression to predict membership renewals. By analyzing customer engagement, purchase history, and reactions to past price adjustments, the model identified at-risk users. The app then launched targeted promotions, such as premium membership discounts, boosting retention rates by 15%.

These models excel at segmentation and targeting, enabling companies to align pricing strategies with customer behavior, thereby improving both customer satisfaction and profitability.

C. Clustering Models: Revealing Hidden Patterns

Clustering models, such as k-means and hierarchical clustering, uncover patterns in data without relying on predefined categories. These models are particularly effective for segmenting customers and discovering trends that can inform tailored pricing strategies.

A hospitality business applied k-means clustering to its booking data, revealing segments like "frequent travelers," "last-minute bookers," and "family vacationers." Using this insight, the company adjusted its pricing accordingly: loyalty discounts for frequent travelers and dynamic premium pricing for last-minute bookings on high-demand dates. This approach increased off-peak bookings by 13%.

It is worth noting that clustering models differ from classification models in that they group data points based on inherent similarities rather than predefined labels. This flexibility allows businesses to uncover unexpected patterns and develop pricing strategies that resonate with specific customer segments.

D. Advanced Models: Tackling Complex Challenges

When dealing with intricate pricing scenarios, advanced models such as random forests, gradient boosting machines, and neural networks offer robust solutions. These models are adept at handling non-linear relationships and high-dimensional datasets, making them ideal for large-scale, complex pricing strategies.

For example, a SaaS company implemented a random forest regression model to predict demand for subscription services. The model integrated diverse factors, including user demographics, engagement metrics, and economic indicators like inflation. Fine-tuning hyperparameters, such as the number of trees and maximum depth, improved the model's accuracy by 22%, enabling the company to refine its tiered pricing plans and enhance customer acquisition.

Despite being computationally intensive, these models master uncovering deep insights in dynamic datasets, making them indispensable for organizations operating in competitive, data-rich environments.

E. Bringing It All Together

Selecting the right AI models for pricing is both an art and a science. It requires aligning business objectives with the unique technical strengths of each model. For instance, regression models excel at precise forecasting, classification supports decision-making, clustering uncovers hidden patterns, and neural networks tackle highly complex scenarios. Each tool serves a distinct purpose, but the challenge lies in finding the best fit for your specific pricing needs, a task that AI itself is beginning to simplify.

Advances in AutoML (Automated Machine Learning) and meta-learning are making AI systems smarter at recommending suitable models for different datasets and goals. These tools analyze data characteristics, problem types, and target outcomes to suggest models reflective of business priorities. For example, an AutoML system might highlight regression for elasticity forecasting or clustering to uncover customer segments for targeted pricing strategies. In some cases, these systems can go beyond recommendations, fine-tuning models for deployment and significantly reducing the manual effort involved.

While AI can streamline model selection, human expertise remains vital in the foreseeable future. AI is good at evaluating technical performance and optimizing parameters, but it may not grasp broader strategic nuances that it has not been trained on. Decisions like balancing accuracy with explainability in regulated industries or aligning pricing strategies with long-term brand goals require human judgment. This blend of computational precision and strategic insight ensures pricing models deliver real-world impact.

The real strength of AI in pricing unfolds when it shifts from being a tool for analysis to a driver of innovation. Properly integrated, AI empowers businesses to move beyond reactive adjustments and embrace proactive strategies that anticipate customer behavior and market dynamics. These systems evolve over time, refining model choices and improving recommendations as new data and trends appear.

In an ever-changing and competitive landscape, this synergy between human insight and AI-driven solutions is decisive. Businesses that apply AI thoughtfully can devise smarter, faster, and more adaptive pricing strategies, paving the way for sustained growth and resilience in uncertain markets.

2. Training the Model: The Stage Where Insights Take Shape

Training an AI model is the pivotal moment when preparation channels into actionable insights. It is the stage where data preparation, feature engineering, and model selection converge, enabling the AI to learn from the patterns and relationships within the data. This process is both exciting and meticulous, often resembling the precision of crafting a complex recipe. Each variable acts as an ingredient, while parameters serve as the seasoning, requiring careful adjustment to achieve the desired result. And, as with any fine-tuned process, it may take multiple iterations to perfect.

In this phase, the AI model scrutinizes the training data to identify patterns that form the foundation for its predictions or decisions. Creating a high-performing model involves rigorous tuning, iterative testing, and performance evaluation to ensure the model generalizes effectively to new, unseen data. At the same time, overfitting, where the model memorizes specific training data rather than learning broader trends, should be avoided.

To illustrate, consider a business using AI to derive optimal product pricing. During training, the model analyzes variables like historical sales data, seasonal trends, and competitor prices. The goal is to uncover patterns that predict how price changes will affect customer demand. But achieving reliable predictions involves experimenting with different algorithms, fine-tuning hyperparameters, and validating the model's accuracy on test data. This iterative process ensures the final model can capture real-world scenarios, delivering actionable and trustworthy pricing recommendations.

By thoughtfully managing the training phase, businesses can turn raw data into a strategic asset, using AI to inform smarter, more adaptive pricing decisions. It is in this stage that the magic truly happens.

A. Starting with Baseline Parameters

Every successful AI model begins with a basic framework, often referred to as baseline parameters. Think of these as your initial draft to test your assumptions and understand the broader structure of your model. At this stage, perfection should not be the goal; rather, you aim to set a functional starting point to recognize early trends and potential issues with your data or approach.

Baseline models serve as a means to get a sense of how the system operates before making more refined adjustments. It is like dipping your toes into the water before taking the plunge, providing you with insights on the data's behavior and helping you determine which adjustments are necessary. By starting with simple, default settings, you streamline the process, allowing room for iterative improvements.

For example, when developing a pricing model for a retail chain, a basic linear regression model with default settings can reveal critical patterns, such as the strong influence of competitor pricing and the lesser impact of seasonal trends. These low-hanging fruits are crucial for guiding subsequent refinements in feature engineering and data enrichment.

Building a baseline model does not require advanced algorithms or deep technical knowledge. It is an uncomplicated step that provides valuable groundwork for more sophisticated iterations. Here is a basic example using Python to illustrate how to start with simple parameters:

```python
from sklearn.linear_model import LinearRegression
from sklearn.model_selection import train_test_split
from sklearn.metrics import mean_squared_error
import pandas as pd

# Load and prepare data
data = pd.read_csv("pricing_data.csv")
X = data[['historical_sales', 'competitor_prices', 'promotions']]
y = data['optimal_price']

# Split into training and testing sets
X_train, X_test, y_train, y_test = train_test_split(X, y, test_size=0.2, random_state=42)

# Train the baseline model
model = LinearRegression()
model.fit(X_train, y_train)
```

```
# Evaluate the model
y_pred = model.predict(X_test)
mse = mean_squared_error(y_test, y_pred)
print(f"Baseline M.ean Squared Error: {mse:.2f}")
```

This simple workflow provides an initial evaluation of the model's performance, helping to pinpoint areas that require refinement. If the baseline model reveals inconsistencies or detects irrelevant features, adjustments can be made to the dataset to improve accuracy.

While baseline models may not produce groundbreaking results, they serve a vital function in the AI development cycle:

Identifying potential gaps: For instance, if predictions do not align with seasonal demand, it suggests the need to include seasonality indicators.

Validating feature significance: If competitor pricing consistently impacts predictions, this signals the need to emphasize it during feature engineering.

Saving time: By revealing fundamental issues early on, baseline models help avoid the time-consuming process of building more complex models that may not improve results until the fundamental data issues are addressed.

Baseline parameters assist in understanding what works, what does not, and where to focus subsequent efforts. Starting simple is not only a practical approach but an essential one. By reflecting on early results and refining strategies, you lay the groundwork for advanced models and more informed pricing decisions.

B. Hyperparameter Tuning

Once the baseline model is up and running, the next step is hyperparameter tuning, a process akin to adjusting the knobs on a sound system. Hyperparameter tuning helps you get the most out of your AI model, enabling it to uncover deeper patterns and nuances in your data.

For example, in a random forest model, the number of trees (n_estimators) impacts both accuracy and computational cost. Too few trees, and the model misses patterns; too many, and it becomes computationally expensive without substantial accuracy gains. Fine-tuning such settings allows the model to strike a balance. There are three typical methods of hyperparameter tuning:

1. Grid Search
   Grid search systematically goes through all possible combinations of predefined parameter values. While thorough, this method can be computationally intensive.

Example: A subscription-based fitness app used grid search to optimize the regularization parameters of a logistic regression model. By narrowing the range of acceptable values, they improved retention predictions by 12%.

2. **Random Search**
   Random search tests randomly chosen combinations of hyperparameters. It is faster than grid search and often delivers comparable results, especially for complex models.

   Example: A SaaS company applied random search to fine-tune a neural network, optimizing layer sizes and activation functions. This approach reduced churn predictions by 10% in half the time required for grid search.

3. **Automated Optimization**
   Advanced tools like Bayesian optimization use probabilistic models to determine the best parameters. These methods streamline tuning by prioritizing the most promising combinations.

   Example: A regional retailer adopted Bayesian optimization to fine-tune their random forest model, achieving a 15% improvement in sales forecast accuracy with minimal computational overhead (Géron 2019).

Here is how you can perform hyperparameter tuning using grid search with scikit-learn:

```python
from sklearn.ensemble import GradientBoostingRegressor
from sklearn.model_selection import GridSearchCV

# Load data
X = data[['historical_sales', 'competitor_prices',
'promotions']]
y = data['optimal_price']

# Define the model
model = GradientBoostingRegressor()

# Define hyperparameter grid
param_grid = {
    'n_estimators': [50, 100, 150],
    'max_depth': [3, 5, 7],
    'learning_rate': [0.01, 0.1, 0.2]
}
```

```
# Perform grid search
grid_search = GridSearchCV(estimator=model, param_grid=param_
grid, cv=5, scoring='neg_mean_squared_error')
grid_search.fit(X, y)

# Best parameters
print(f"Best Parameters: {grid_search.best_params_}")
```

This script evaluates different combinations of n_estimators, max_depth, and learning_rate, selecting the combination that minimizes prediction error.

Hyperparameter tuning is an iterative process that demands patience but pays off with significant performance gains. Small adjustments to hyperparameters can lead to dramatic improvements in prediction accuracy or efficiency. Fine-tuned models can better capture nuances, making them more adaptable to dynamic, real-world environments. Hyperparameter tuning is not simply about improving a model; the ultimate goal is to craft a solution that fits your unique pricing challenges and unlocking its full potential.

C. Evaluate on Testing Data

Once your model has been trained, it is time to see how well it performs in the real world, or at least, in a simulated version of it. Evaluation is the moment of truth, where your carefully constructed model faces new, unseen data. It is a bit like experimenting a new recipe on guests. You hope it impresses, but it might need a few tweaks before it is perfect.

Evaluating on testing data ensures your model can generalize, meaning it can perform well not just on the data it was trained on but also on new scenarios. Without this step, you risk creating a model that's overfitted, memorizing the training data instead of learning meaningful patterns.

The process involves feeding your testing dataset into the trained model and comparing the model's predictions to the actual outcomes. For pricing applications, the stakes are high: an underperforming model could lead to lost revenue or dissatisfied customers. Evaluation metrics vary depending on the type of model you are using:

- For regression models, **Mean Squared Error (MSE)** measures the average squared difference between predicted and actual values. Smaller values indicate better predictions.

- For classification models, metrics like **accuracy**, **precision**, and **recall** gauge how effectively the model categorizes data. These are especially useful for binary decisions like whether a customer will accept a price increase.
- For clustering models, the **Silhouette Score** evaluates how well-defined and distinct the identified clusters are.

Evaluating a regression model on testing data typically involves calculating key metrics like MSE. Here is an example using Python:

```
from sklearn.ensemble import RandomForestRegressor
from sklearn.model_selection import train_test_split
from sklearn.metrics import mean_squared_error
import pandas as pd

# Load data
data = pd.read_csv("pricing_data.csv")
X = data[['demand', 'competitor_prices', 'seasonal_index']]
y = data['optimal_price']

# Split data into training and testing sets
X_train, X_test, y_train, y_test = train_test_split(X, y,
test_size=0.2, random_state=42)

# Train the model
model = RandomForestRegressor(n_estimators=100, random_state=42)
model.fit(X_train, y_train)

# Evaluate the model
y_pred = model.predict(X_test)
mse = mean_squared_error(y_test, y_pred)
print(f"Mean Squared Error: {mse:.2f}")
```

This process reveals discrepancies between predicted and actual outcomes, guiding adjustments to improve the model.

Model evaluation is not a one-and-done task. Metrics like MSE (Mean Squared Error), accuracy, and Silhouette Scores serve as guideposts, revealing where the model excels and where it struggles. However, interpreting these metrics is crucial for understanding model performance beyond just the numbers. For example, a low MSE indicates that the model's predictions are close to actual values, but we have to ensure that the model is not overfitting to noise or outliers. Accuracy, though often used as a general indicator, can be misleading in imbalanced datasets, where high accuracy may be achieved by predicting the majority class (i.e., the class label that has the most instances in a dataset for a classification problem). In such cases, additional metrics like precision, recall, and F1 score offer more insight into performance, especially in the case of rare events or anomalies.

Silhouette Scores, commonly used in clustering tasks, measure how well each point fits within its assigned cluster. A higher Silhouette Score suggests that the model has formed distinct and meaningful groups, while a lower score could indicate that the clusters are poorly defined or overlapping.

Iteration is king. Refining the model based on these insights can significantly enhance its performance. Evaluation is not just about the raw scores but understanding what they reveal about the model's behavior, revealing areas where adjustments are necessary.

Evaluation bridges the gap between theoretical modeling and practical application. It ensures that your AI pricing system not only works on paper but also delivers value in real-world scenarios. By carefully testing and iterating, you can build a robust model that adapts to dynamic market conditions, aligns with customer expectations, and resulting in improved financial performance.

D. Iterating and Improving the Model

Model training is a reiterative process. If training a model is like cooking up a new recipe, iterating on it is where the real mastery happens. You have got a dish that's edible, maybe even enjoyable, but with a few tweaks, it could be exceptional. This step zeroes in on refining your AI model, testing, learning, and adjusting until it performs as consistently and accurately as possible.

Iteration is the beating heart of successful AI implementation. Even the most robust model can rarely address every challenge on its first run. Market conditions change, customer behaviors evolve, and sometimes, initial assumptions turn out to be flawed. That is why iteration is essential for building a model that stays relevant and effective over time.

The first version of your model produces valuable insights, not just about its predictions but also about the data it was trained on and the assumptions built into its design. Often, these early runs highlight surprising patterns or gaps that were not obvious before. Take, for example, a regional airline that deployed a dynamic pricing model for seat bookings. While the model performed well in the beginning, post-launch analysis revealed that it struggled with weekend travel demand. By examining its predictions and revisiting the dataset, the team realized that weekday and weekend booking patterns differed significantly, requiring separate feature sets for each. This discovery would not have come without iteration.

Improving a model means an opportunity to experiment, tweaking parameters, adding new features, or even testing alternative models. Iteration also involves adjusting features. You might discover that external factors like regional holidays or competitor promotions have a stronger influence on customer behavior than previously thought. Incorporating these variables can significantly improve the model's efficacy.

Version control systems like **DVC (Data Version Control)** help track changes to datasets and models, ensuring reproducibility. Automated machine learning (AutoML) platforms like H2O.ai and Google's AutoML can streamline experimentation, suggesting model improvements based on early results.

Hyperparameter tuning methods, such as **Bayesian optimization**, also play an important part during iteration. By systematically exploring the parameter space, these techniques uncover settings that balance accuracy, efficiency, and interpretability.

Iteration is best approached as a series of manageable experiments rather than sweeping overhauls. For each cycle:

1. Analyze the model's performance on testing and validation data.
2. Identify specific weaknesses or unexpected patterns.
3. Adjust parameters, features, or even the choice of algorithm to address these issues.
4. Retrain and re-evaluate the model to measure improvement.

Below is an example of training and evaluating a random forest regression model using Python:

```
from sklearn.ensemble import RandomForestRegressor
from sklearn.model_selection import GridSearchCV

# Load and split data
X = data[['demand', 'competitor_prices', 'seasonal_index']]
y = data['optimal_price']
X_train, X_test, y_train, y_test = train_test_split(X, y,
test_size=0.2, random_state=42)

# Define the baseline model
model = RandomForestRegressor(random_state=42)
```

```
# Iterative improvement with grid search
param_grid = {
    'n_estimators': [100, 200, 300],
    'max_depth': [None, 10, 20],
    'min_samples_split': [2, 5, 10]
}
grid_search = GridSearchCV(estimator=model, param_grid=param_
grid, cv=5, scoring='neg_mean_squared_error')
grid_search.fit(X_train, y_train)

# Evaluate the best model
best_model = grid_search.best_estimator_
y_pred = best_model.predict(X_test)
mse = mean_squared_error(y_test, y_pred)
print(f"Improved Mean Squared Error: {mse:.2f}")
```

This iterative process improves the model's performance by systematically testing parameter combinations and selecting the best-performing configuration. Iteration is where the magic of AI truly shines, pushing the boundaries of what is possible. Each cycle of refinement brings you closer to a model that fulfills your pricing objectives and adapts to the nuances of your market.

3. Balancing Experimentation with Precision: Training AI Models

Model training combines elements of both creativity and systematic analysis. It involves constant experimentation, iterative refinements, and learning from setbacks. Rarely does a model perform perfectly on its first run. However, through careful adjustments and persistent effort, businesses can make the best of what AI has to offer.

Consider the earlier example of the hospitality client. Initially, their AI model struggled with inconsistent predictions. By refining the model's parameters and incorporating new features, such as accounting for seasonal trends, they finally achieved a breakthrough. The updated model not only enhanced booking rates but also enriched insights into customer preferences, paving the way for more targeted marketing and pricing strategies.

The key to successful AI-enabled pricing lies in aligning the chosen model with the business' unique objectives and the dataset's characteristics. The most complex or cutting-edge algorithm may not be the best solution. What makes the difference is being mindful about selecting and training the model that best suits the problem at hand. With the right techniques, businesses can use AI to deliver smarter, faster, and more responsive pricing strategies. This adaptability leads to tangible benefits like improved profitability, stronger customer relationships, and a competitive edge in an increasingly dynamic marketplace.

Phase 3: Scaling AI Solutions—From Pilot Project to Organization-Wide Deployment

This is where the rubber meets the road. You have built your AI model, trialed it with test data, and are ready to roll it out. But implementation often throws unexpected curveballs.

Take the case of a nationwide grocery chain that piloted dynamic pricing for perishable goods. The initial results were astounding, as they managed to reduce food waste by 15% and boosted sales by 10%. Yet, when they announced plans to scale the program, store managers pushed back. "AI can't possibly understand our customers like we do," one manager protested during a meeting.

The leadership team did not dismiss these concerns right away. Instead, they took the time to communicate how the AI system worked and emphasized that managers could still override its recommendations. This collaborative approach turned skeptics into advocates, paving the way for a successful company-wide rollout.

Scaling AI is as much about building trust as about deploying software. It is important for your team to understand that AI is not here to replace them. It is here to make their jobs easier and more impactful. Implementation and scaling are about turning that sleek prototype into a reliable workhorse that fits seamlessly into your organization's workflows. And just like driving, implementing AI pricing solutions comes with its bumps in the road.

1. The Challenges of Implementation

Bringing AI into pricing will not be a plug-and-play process. It is transformative but often complicated. While the potential rewards are immense, the path to successful implementation is paved with challenges. Let's explore what makes this journey tricky and how businesses can navigate these obstacles effectively.

A. Integration with Existing Systems

One of the most significant hurdles is integrating AI into a tangled web of legacy systems. Many companies rely on disparate platforms for sales, inventory, and customer data, which often do not communicate effectively. Implementing AI in such fragmented ecosystems requires careful planning and often significant investment.

For example, a retailer implementing dynamic pricing discovered that their inventory management system lacked real-time updates. This misalignment created issues where online discounts promoted by the AI model did not reflect actual stock availability in stores, frustrating customers. To resolve this, the company adopted a middleware platform to synchronize its systems, enabling a seamless flow of data and improving operational efficiency (Linardatos et al. 2020).

Integration can be tedious and painful. Businesses must evaluate their existing infrastructure, identify gaps, and prioritize investments in scalable solutions that foster system interoperability.

B. Resistance to Change

AI offers the potential for smarter pricing strategies, but its adoption often faces resistance. Teams accustomed to traditional manual processes may worry about losing control or making costly mistakes, and the idea of relying on algorithms for complex pricing decisions can seem impersonal and counterproductive.

For example, a consumer goods company implemented an AI-enabled promotional tool, but initial resistance from the sales team almost derailed the project. Many of them saw the algorithm as a threat to their expertise. To address these concerns, company leaders involved sales representatives early in the development phase, incorporating their input to refine the AI system. Additionally, they shared the results from a pilot program, which showed a 12% improvement in promotion efficiency, to help build trust and garner support for scaling the solution (Davenport and Ronanki 2018).

Gaining acceptance for AI requires both transparency and collaboration. Starting with small-scale trials that showcase clear benefits can help foster confidence and support across different teams.

C. Ensuring Data Privacy

Data privacy is an essential aspect of implementing AI, particularly with regulations like the General Data Protection Regulation (GDPR) in the European Union and the California Consumer Privacy Act (CCPA). These regulations impose strict guidelines on how data should be collected, processed, and stored, and non-compliance can result in severe penalties.

For example, an e-commerce subscription platform aiming to personalize pricing struggled with balancing AI innovation and data privacy requirements. To cope with these challenges, they incorporated anonymization methods and federated learning, enabling the training of AI models using decentralized data sources. This strategy allowed them to comply with privacy regulations while retaining the efficacy of their models (Rieke et al. 2020).

To ensure compliance, organizations should engage legal teams early in the AI development process and implement privacy-preserving methods such as differential privacy or secure multiparty computation. Additionally, clear, and transparent communication with customers about data usage helps build trust and strengthen customer loyalty.

D. Navigating the Roadblocks

Implementing AI-enabled pricing can be a daunting task. From integrating new AI tools with legacy systems to overcoming resistance from teams, as well as ensuring adherence to strict data privacy regulations, the process can be overwhelming. However, these challenges present valuable opportunities to lay a more robust and flexible foundation for future innovation.

One of the first obstacles often faced has to do with integration. Many organizations continue to rely on outdated systems that do not seamlessly interact with modern technology. Another significant barrier is resistance to change. Teams that are accustomed to manual decision-making may view AI with doubt. In one example, a manufacturing company eased concerns by implementing AI gradually, starting with a pilot program that clearly proved its value. Transparent communication and involving key stakeholders in the process helped turn initial skeptics into advocates for the technology (Davenport and Ronanki 2018). Additionally, data privacy remains a critical consideration. Organizations must comply with regulations like GDPR and CCPA while still making use of valuable customer insights.

These challenges, while significant, are far from insurmountable. Overcoming them requires not just technology upgrades, but a shift in organizational mindset and policy. Companies that view these challenges as opportunities for growth and refinement are better positioned to fully harness the potential of AI-enabled pricing.

2. In-House vs. Outsourcing: Choosing the Right Path

Choosing whether to develop an AI-enabled pricing solution in-house or to outsource the project is a critical decision for any organization. This choice is analogous to deciding whether to conduct a home renovation project independently or hire a professional contractor. Both options offer distinct advantages and challenges, and the right decision often hinges on factors such as the company's specific goals, available resources, and timeline.

Building an AI pricing solution in-house provides the benefit of full control and customization, enabling the organization to adapt the system precisely to its needs. However, this path requires considerable investment in time, expertise, and infrastructure, which can be a challenge for companies without a dedicated data science team (Davenport and Ronanki 2018). Conversely, outsourcing AI development may save time and resources by tapping into external expertise. However, this approach may present challenges in aligning the solution with the company's unique needs and raise concerns about data security and a potential loss of control over the technology.

A. *The Case for In-House Development*

Developing an AI pricing system in-house offers the significant advantage of complete control over its design and functionality. Organizations can tailor the system precisely to their needs, integrate it seamlessly with their existing infrastructure, and retain ownership of intellectual property. For businesses with specialized markets or complex operational requirements, this level of customization can provide a critical edge.

Consider the example of a global retailer that opted to develop its pricing solution internally. With a professional team comprising data scientists, machine learning engineers, and industry specialists, the company crafted a solution that perfectly complemented its proprietary e-commerce platform. Although the initial investment in talent and technology was substantial, the resulting system surpassed generic alternatives in both performance and strategic value, offering the company a competitive advantage (Brownlee 2019). Moreover, the expertise developed during the project was later transferred to enhance other business operations, such as inventory control and customer segmentation.

Despite its advantages, in-house development can be demanding. It requires highly specialized technical skills, substantial financial investment, and a lengthy development process. For smaller businesses or those new to AI, the complexity and cost of building an AI system internally may outweigh the benefits, making this approach less viable for certain organizations (Davenport and Ronanki 2018).

B. The Case for Outsourcing

Outsourcing can be an appealing option for organizations that aim to implement AI quickly or lack the necessary internal expertise to develop a sophisticated pricing system. By collaborating with specialized vendors, companies gain access to advanced technologies, industry best practices, and the expertise of experienced professionals, all without the challenge of building the system from scratch.

For instance, a regional airline decided to outsource its dynamic pricing solution to a SaaS provider specializing in travel-related technologies. The system was up and running in just three months, adjusting ticket prices in real time based on booking patterns and competitor pricing. As a result, the airline saw a 12% increase in revenue per passenger mile. However, the company had to deal with headaches such as ongoing subscription fees and limited flexibility to adjust the system as their business needs evolved (Heaton 2017a).

While outsourcing offers rapid deployment and efficiency, it also introduces risks such as a lack of control over system customization and potential vendor dependency. To mitigate these risks, companies should thoroughly assess service agreements, ensure they retain data ownership, and partner with vendors that provide scalable and flexible solutions.

C. Key Considerations for Decision-Making

When deciding between in-house development and outsourcing for your AI pricing solution, we should carefully evaluate the following factors:

1. Scale and Complexity of Your Needs:
   Businesses with specialized pricing strategies or complex integration requirements might find that in-house development offers more tailored solutions. In contrast, if your pricing needs are more standardized, outsourcing can provide a quicker and more cost-effective solution (Davenport and Ronanki 2018).
2. Budget and Resources:
   Developing an AI solution in-house requires significant initial investment in talent, technology, and infrastructure. Outsourcing, however, may lower the upfront costs but can involve ongoing fees and potentially reduced flexibility in adapting the system to changing needs (Loukides 2020a, b).
3. Timeline:
   Outsourcing typically accelerates the implementation process, making it ideal for businesses seeking immediate solutions. In-house development, however, takes more time, as it requires the design, development, and refinement of the system over a longer period (Brynjolfsson and McAfee 2014).
4. Long-Term Goals:
   For companies aiming to build in-house AI expertise for broader applications, developing the system internally aligns with long-term strategic objectives. On the other hand, outsourcing might limit opportunities for internal knowledge transfer, which could hinder the development of internal capabilities over time (Davenport and Ronanki 2018).

In practice, it is not uncommon to choose a hybrid approach by outsourcing the initial phase of development, then gradually transitioning to in-house management as their internal teams gain experience. For example, a telecommunications company partnered with an external vendor to implement an AI-powered pricing solution but simultaneously used the collaboration to train their in-house team. Over time, the company was able to take over the management of the system independently, reducing reliance on the vendor while keeping a custom solution (Davenport and Ronanki 2018).

There is no universal solution to the in-house versus outsourcing dilemma. The ideal choice depends on your organization's specific requirements, resources, and long-term goals. The key is to make a decision that aligns with your business strategy and sets you up for success in the evolving AI-enabled pricing landscape.

3. Best Practices for Implementation

Regardless of whether you choose in-house development or outsourcing, the effectiveness of AI pricing implementation depends on following a structured approach. By adhering to best practices, businesses can facilitate smoother adoption, minimize operational disruptions, and maximize the potential benefits AI offers to pricing strategies. Below are key best practices for successful AI implementation:

A. Start with a Pilot

A critical first step when introducing AI into pricing is starting small by launching a pilot project within a specific market, product line, or channel. This controlled environment enables businesses to refine the model, uncover potential challenges, and assess the return on investment (ROI) before scaling.

For example, a fitness app that offers premium memberships launched an AI-enabled pricing solution targeting users who were highly engaged but hesitant to upgrade. By using predictive analytics to offer personalized discounts, the app increased premium sign-ups by 20% during the pilot. Encouraged by these results, the company expanded the AI system to include upselling strategies and churn prevention across all membership tiers.

Pilots are useful to assess the system's effectiveness and provide the opportunity to address issues before scaling. Moreover, they build organizational confidence by showing tangible, positive outcomes early in the process (Davenport and Ronanki 2018).

B. Involve Cross-Functional Teams

Pricing is not a standalone function; it connects multiple areas of an organization, such as sales, marketing, and finance. Effective implementation requires collaboration among these departments to ensure the AI solution aligns with the overall business strategy and meets the needs of various stakeholders.

Take, for instance, a global retail company that decided to deploy a dynamic pricing system. Rather than leaving the project solely in the hands of the data science team, they involved key members from marketing and sales. The marketing team shed light on seasonal demand fluctuations that the AI model initially overlooked, while the sales team contributed valuable insights on customer purchasing behaviors. This collaboration resulted in a pricing model that was more in line with actual market conditions, leading to a 15% increase in revenue (Davenport and Ronanki 2018).

Engaging cross-functional teams fosters smoother AI integration within organizational workflows, addresses existing pain points, and enhances the likelihood of broader acceptance across the business (Chui et al. 2018).

C. Continuously Monitor Performance

AI models are built to evolve and grow better over time. A frequent pitfall is assuming that once an AI system is implemented, it requires no further attention. In fact, ongoing monitoring is crucial to ensure the model continues to meet business objectives and remains responsive to shifts in market dynamics.

One of the best practices in this process is establishing clear key performance indicators (KPIs) to assess the AI's performance. Metrics like margin improvements, increases in conversion rates, and overall revenue growth provide tangible evidence of the model's impact. For instance, a ride-hailing company initially noticed higher fares during off-peak times after introducing dynamic pricing. By closely checking elasticity metrics, the company realized the need to adjust pricing for low-demand periods, leading to more balanced pricing and improved customer satisfaction and retention (Heaton 2017b).

Regular performance evaluations are also necessary for determining when the model needs retraining or additional adjustments to stay competitive in a changing marketplace.

D. Prepare for Iteration

Realistically, the first iteration of your AI model is unlikely to be perfect. Do not panic or get frustrated. Treat implementation as a continuous learning process rather than a one-time project. Iteration is the cornerstone of long-term success, allowing the model to evolve with your business needs.

For example, a logistics company rolled out an AI-powered freight pricing model. Initial performance was promising, but the system struggled to account for rapid fluctuations in fuel prices. By incorporating this data into subsequent iterations and fine-tuning hyperparameters, the model improved accuracy by 18%, leading to better profitability during volatile periods (Rieke et al. 2020).

Iteration does not only fix bugs but also uncover new opportunities for improvement. By regularly updating the model with fresh data and feedback, you ensure it remains a valuable asset over time. It would be a pity to negate the efficacy of the AI model without revisiting underlying parameters, which might have undergone changes that were not initially accounted for. Continuous evaluation helps adapt the model to evolving conditions, ensuring it stays in touch with current realities and business objectives.

E. Put It All Together

Once an AI pricing solution has proven its worth, the next significant step is scaling it across the entire organization. Scaling is not just about applying the system to new markets or product categories but also about weaving AI into the fabric of the company's decision-making processes. It requires thoughtful strategy, a focus on customization to meet specific business needs, and a strong emphasis on educating employees on how to use AI-enabled insights effectively (Chui et al. 2020). Successful scaling involves ensuring that the system is fully integrated into everyday operations and becomes an essential tool for pricing decisions across all levels of the business.

4. Scaling Across the Organization

Demonstrating the effectiveness of your AI pricing solution is merely the beginning of the journey. The real test lies in scaling it across the entire organization. Scaling does not merely involve applying the solution to new markets or product categories. It requires integrating AI into the organization's decision-making culture, making it a core component of everyday operations (Brynjolfsson and McAfee 2017). Scaling requires careful planning, customization to meet specific business needs, and the training of teams to make the best of AI-generated insights.

A. Embrace Automation

A key enabler for successful scaling is automation. Leveraging cloud platforms and advanced AI technologies allows companies to automate routine tasks, such as updating pricing models or providing real-time recommendations. This reduces manual workload and ensures that pricing decisions remain consistent and accurate.

Automation not only increases operational efficiency but also guarantees that pricing models are always informed by the most recent data, improving the quality and speed of decision-making on a larger scale (Chui et al. 2020).

B. Tailor AI to Local Markets

AI models are incredibly powerful, but they are not universally applicable across all markets. Every market comes with distinct customer preferences, competitive dynamics, and regulatory requirements, making it crucial to adjust your pricing models accordingly.

Consider the example of a global e-commerce retailer that expanded its AI-enabled pricing solution. While dynamic discounts targeting budget-conscious consumers worked well in North America, the company found that Southeast Asian markets required a more nuanced approach. There, smaller, more personalized promotions resonated better due to heightened price sensitivity. By customizing their AI pricing model for each region, the company achieved greater revenue, preserved customer trust, and complied with local regulations (Kumar and Shah 2021).

Customizing AI systems to fit local market conditions is mandatory for the system's success. It enhances the effectiveness of pricing strategies, improves adoption, and ensures that businesses are responsive to regional market dynamics (Lee 2019).

C. Educate the Teams

It may have become obvious that AI goes beyond a set of technological tools and requires collaboration between advanced systems and human expertise. For AI to be successfully scaled, it is essential to equip sales, marketing, and pricing teams with the knowledge to understand and act on AI-enabled insights. Without fostering this understanding, even the most sophisticated models can fall short of their potential.

For example, a telecommunications company implementing an AI-based pricing solution encountered resistance from its regional teams, who were unfamiliar with AI tools. To address this, the company developed an extensive training program designed to demystify the AI system. The training focused on explaining how the AI generated its recommendations, along with highlighting its practical benefits through real-world case studies. Following the training, internal surveys revealed a 30% increase in team confidence and engagement with AI insights, leading to a more effective and smoother scaling process (Brynjolfsson and McAfee 2017; Hagel 2020).

Investing in education is indispensable to ensure that AI is not only adopted but embraced across the organization. When teams can successfully integrate their expertise with AI insights, the overall effectiveness of AI-enabled strategies improves, promoting long-term success.

D. Painting a Big Picture

Scaling AI throughout an organization extends beyond merely deploying technology; it is about fostering an innovative culture. Effective implementation of AI pricing solutions hinges on automation to optimize operations, customization to ensure market relevance, and education to promote trust and widespread adoption (Brynjolfsson and McAfee 2017). By aligning these elements, companies will enhance growth potential and maintain a competitive edge in the marketplace.

Furthermore, this holistic approach improves the chances that AI-enabled pricing solutions are seamlessly integrated into business processes, providing long-term value. When automation is strategically applied, and teams are educated and engaged, the organization is positioned to reap the full benefits of AI while fostering continuous innovation (Davenport and Westerman 2018).

5. A Human Aspect of Scaling AI

While the technical aspects of scaling AI are crucial, the human element often proves to be the most challenging, and ultimately, the most significant, an integral part of the process. It is not just about implementing a system; it is about integrating that system into the culture and operations of the company in a way that nurtures trust, engagement, and acceptance of humans that work with AI.

BrightMart, a mid-sized grocery chain, faced exactly this challenge. After running a successful AI pricing pilot in one of its urban locations, the company saw a significant boost in revenue, as dynamic pricing helped reduce food waste by 15% while improving sales. Buoyed by this success, the leadership team decided to roll out the AI system across all stores. However, store managers were skeptical, who were used to relying on their intuition and experience for pricing. They doubted whether the AI could capture the nuances of customer behavior. One manager even voiced, "How can an algorithm understand that Mrs. Carter always buys her peaches on Tuesdays and will pay full price if they look fresh?"

The leadership team quickly recognized that successfully scaling the AI solution hinged on addressing human concerns and fostering trust. They focused on transparency, walking store managers through the AI system during regional meetings and explaining how the tool worked, from the data it analyzed to the pricing decisions it recommended. They acknowledged the system's limitations, explaining how it might miss local nuances such as a sudden farmers' market that could impact sales.

The shift in tone was noticeable. Managers, initially hesitant, became more open to the idea, asking questions like, "If I see a mistake, can I override it?" When assured that they could, the atmosphere relaxed. The leadership team then focused the next phase of the rollout on regions where managers were more receptive to the system, celebrating every single win down the road. For example, one store reduced food waste by 15% thanks to AI-enabled markdown suggestions, which quickly became a story shared across the organization. Another store experimented with bakery item discounts during slower hours, leading to increased sales and higher customer satisfaction.

The breakthrough came when BrightMart's leadership emphasized that AI was not supposed to replace human judgment but to enhance it. By allowing managers to adjust the AI's recommendations, the system became a trusted advisor, not an inflexible rule enforcer. One manager reflected, "I thought AI would take control away from me, but it is more like a second opinion, a really fast one. It is still my call, and that makes all the difference."

Scaling AI is not just about deploying technology; it is about people in the end. Trust and buy-in from the team are built through transparency, collaboration, and an acknowledgment of the expertise that exists within the organization long before AI arrived (Brynjolfsson and McAfee 2017).

Scaling AI effectively requires telling a story, one where successes, no matter how small, are celebrated, and where the AI system is presenters as a partner rather than a replacement. When you focus on the human side of the equation, you set the stage for greater success and broader acceptance of AI tools within your organization. By empowering employees with the right tools and involving them in the process, AI becomes a catalyst for growth and a driver of confidence across the company.

6. The Road to Transformative AI-Enabled Pricing

The journey from implementing AI-powered pricing systems to scaling them across an entire organization is both challenging and immensely rewarding. It represents a transformation that touches upon every facet of the business, influencing how teams collaborate, think, and make strategic decisions. Achieving success in this area requires a combination of vision, persistence, and adaptability, whether developing a solution in-house or partnering with external experts (Chui et al. 2021).

AI is a tool, not a miracle cure. The companies that successfully implement AI-enabled pricing are those that clearly define their objectives, whether it is enhancing customer satisfaction, improving margins, or gaining a competitive advantage (Brynjolfsson and McAfee 2014). Without this vision, even the most advanced AI systems can become costly experiments with unclear outcomes.

However, having a clear goal is just the beginning. Collaboration is often where the true transformation happens. Pricing is not an isolated function; it intersects with sales, marketing, operations, and customer service, among others. Successful implementation requires breaking down silos and fostering a collaborative environment. Experience shows that cross-functional workshops, where stakeholders align on shared priorities and challenges, have proven essential to smooth adoption and effective integration (Davenport and Ronanki 2018).

Naturally, the path to success is lined with challenges. Resistance to change is natural, especially when AI challenges established processes and human intelligence. I recall a situation where store managers in a retail environment were initially resistant to dynamic pricing models. It was not until leadership positioned AI as a support tool, rather than a replacement, that trust began to build. The team involved managers early in the process, demonstrating how their input shaped the AI's pricing recommendations. This approach, which emphasized human involvement, turned skeptics into advocates and facilitated a smoother rollout (Binns 2018).

Then there is the challenge of scaling, which is often underestimated. Scaling an AI solution is not just about deploying the technology; it is more about integrating AI into the decision-making culture of the organization. This requires automating workflows where feasible while still allowing space for human judgment. It also involves continuous investment in education, helping teams understand how to use AI insights effectively and with confidence (Chui et al. 2021).

Iteration is key to long-term success. No AI implementation is flawless from the start. The companies that thrive are those that treat AI as a continuously evolving capability. They set up feedback loops, regularly reassessing and refining models to keep them aligned with changing business needs. This iterative approach distinguishes successful early adopters from those who struggle after their initial deployment (Davenport and Ronanki 2018).

The true transformation comes not only from tangible results such as higher profit margins or better customer experiences but from the mindset shift that AI fosters across an organization. AI nudges teams to think bigger, act faster, and work with greater precision. Pricing, once seen as a reactive task, evolves into a strategic lever for growth and innovation (Brynjolfsson and McAfee 2014).

The potential of AI in pricing is vast. Equipped with AI, companies will be able to predict and proactively manage market forces. They can predict customer needs, experiment with bold strategies, and make faster, smarter decisions. The rewards outweigh the effort. While the path to AI-enabled pricing may not always be easy, the success stories from businesses that have already embarked on this journey highlight its immense value.

As you continue on or begin your journey toward AI-enabled pricing, remember that success does not come from perfect execution alone. It stems from resilience, collaboration, and a commitment to continuous learning. By embracing flexibility and a willingness to adapt, you unlock not only the power of AI but the full potential of your teams and your business (Davenport and Ronanki 2018).

References

Bae S, Kim J, Lee H (2023) Advances in AI-enabled pricing: tools and platforms for managing big data. J Digit Innov 45(2):56–72

Bertsimas D, Kallus N (2020) From predictive to prescriptive analytics. Manag Sci 66(3):1–23. https://doi.org/10.1287/mnsc.2019.3531

Binns A (2018) Responsible AI: a framework for building trust in your AI solutions. Deloitte Insights. https://www2.deloitte.com/content/dam/insights/us/articles/4514_AI-ethics/4514_AIEthics.pdf

Binns T (2021) How generative AI is transforming pricing strategies. AI Business Review. https://www.aibusinessreview.com

Brownlee J (2019) Machine learning mastery. Machine Learning Mastery

Brynjolfsson E, McAfee A (2014) The second machine age: work, progress, and prosperity in a time of brilliant technologies. W.W. Norton & Company

Brynjolfsson E, McAfee A (2017) The second machine age: Work, progress, and prosperity in a time of brilliant technologies. W.W. Norton & Company

Built In (2023) Generative AI in SaaS pricing: a case study of GPT-based simulations. Built In. https://builtin.com

Chen L, Zhao Y (2019) Machine learning for dynamic pricing: forecasting and optimal pricing strategies. J Bus Anal 8(2):123–139. https://doi.org/10.1016/j.jba.2019.02.001

Chen J, Zhang X, Li Y (2020) The role of data quality in AI-powered pricing systems. J Bus Anal 15(4):200–214. https://doi.org/10.1016/j.jba.2020.07.002

Chen Y, Zhang C, Goh M (2021) Data integration in AI systems: Insights from cloud-based platforms. J Bus Intell 34(2):45–59

Choi E, Schuetz A, Safavi M (2021) Data privacy and the future of AI-enabled business intelligence: a study of synthetic data generation. J Bus Anal 9(3):165–179. https://doi.org/10.1016/j.jba.2021.02.005

Choudhury M, Bharadwaj A, Bhatnagar S (2022) Consumer behavior in digital ecosystems: implications for pricing and demand forecasting. J Market Sci 40(1):78–92

Chui M, Manyika J, Miremadi M (2018) Harnessing automation for a future that works. McKinsey Global Institute

Chui M, Manyika J, Miremadi M (2020) The next normal in AI adoption: the road to a responsible and efficient future. McKinsey & Company

Chui M, Manyika J, Miremadi M (2021) The state of AI in 2021. McKinsey & Company. https://www.mckinsey.com/featured-insights/artificial-intelligence/the-state-of-ai-in-2021

Datamatics. (2024). A global beverage giant registers significant volume gains across categories by leveraging AI/ML models for managing price elasticities. Datamatics Case Studies. https://www.datamatics.com/resources/case-studies/a-global-beverage-giant-registers-significant-volume-gains-across-categories-by-leveraging-ai/ml-models-for-managing-price-elasticities

Davenport TH, Bean R (2020) AI in pricing: How artificial intelligence is transforming business strategies. Harvard Business Review Press

Davenport TH, Ronanki R (2018) Artificial intelligence for the real world. Harv Bus Rev 96(1):108–116. https://hbr.org/2018/01/artificial-intelligence-for-the-real-world

Davenport TH, Westerman G (2018) How artificial intelligence will impact the future of marketing. MIT Sloan Manag Rev 59(4):22–29

Devabit (2023) 11 new technologies in AI: Trends of 2023–2024. Devabit. Retrieved from https://www.devabit.com

Emerald Insight (2023a) AI-enabled pricing: Lessons from early adopters in retail. Retrieved from https://www.emeraldinsight.com

Emerald Insight (2023b) Artificial intelligence and pricing. Retrieved from https://www.emerald.com

EY (2023a) The art of pricing in the age of AI. Retrieved from https://www.ey.com

EY (2023b) Enhancing profitability through data-driven pricing strategies

Géron A (2019) Hands-on machine learning with Scikit-Learn, Keras, and TensorFlow. O'Reilly Media

Gilpin LH, Bau D, Yuan BZ, Melamed T (2018) Explaining explanations: an overview of interpretability of machine learning. Proceedings of the 2018 CHI conference on human factors in computing systems, 1–11. https://doi.org/10.1145/3173574.3173578

Hagel J (2020) The collaboration imperative: unlocking AI's potential in business strategy. Harv Bus Rev 98(2):34–45

Heaton J (2017a) Deep learning and AI in business applications. Addison-Wesley

Heaton J (2017b) Introduction to machine learning with Python. O'Reilly Media

Human-Centered AI Institute at Stanford University (2023) 2023 AI index report. Stanford HAI. https://hai.stanford.edu/ai-index/2023-ai-index-report

IBM (2023) AI-powered pricing optimization: How machine learning drives pricing decisions. IBM Watson. https://www.ibm.com/watson

Jain R, Sharma P (2021) Managing big data for business growth: strategies for leveraging AI in pricing. Int J Bus Intell 12(4):105–118

Johnson M, Evans A, Lee P (2020) Enhancing e-commerce with dynamic pricing strategies: an AI-based approach. J Retail Analyt 16(1):54–67. https://doi.org/10.1016/j.jra.2019.11.007

Joulin A, Grave E, Mikolov T, Van den Oord A (2017) Bag of tricks for efficient text classification. arXiv:1607.01759. https://arxiv.org/abs/1607.01759

KDnuggets (2023a) What to expect for AI quality trends in 2023. Retrieved from https://www.kdnuggets.com

KDnuggets (2023b) AI in logistics and pricing optimization. Retrieved from https://www.kdnuggets.com

Kumar A, Shah D (2021) Global pricing strategies: the challenges of customization in diverse markets. J Int Bus Strat 15(3):56–72

Lee S (2019) Adapting AI pricing models to regional market nuances: Best practices for global scaling. Int J Pricing Strat 10(4):22–35

Lee J, Choi Y, Kim J (2021) The role of natural language processing in enhancing dynamic pricing strategies. Int J Bus AI 12(2):111–128. https://doi.org/10.1177/2147483647

Linardatos P, Papastefanopoulos V, Kotsiantis S (2020) Explainable AI: a review of machine learning interpretability methods. Entropy (Basel, Switzerland) 23(1):18

Little RJA, Rubin DB (2020) Statistical analysis with missing data, 3rd edn. Wiley

Liu Y, Chen S (2020) Personalized promotions powered by generative AI. Journal of Marketing Innovation 58(2):109–123

Liu Y, Wang C, Xie Y (2018) Exploring trends in consumer sentiment through social media for pricing strategies. J Mark Res 55(6):811–825. https://doi.org/10.1509/jmr.17.0360

Loukides M (2020a) Data Science for Business: a Guide for Data-Driven Decision Making. O'Reilly Media

Loukides M (2020b) The data-driven future: preparing for AI's challenges and opportunities. O'Reilly Media

Marr B (2018) How Walmart is using machine learning, AI, and big data to boost performance. Forbes. Retrieved from https://www.forbes.com

Martinez E, Liao F (2021) AI-enabled pricing models: transforming the landscape. Int J Pricing Res 32(4):294–312

McKinsey & Company (2023, March 5) How personalized pricing drives loyalty and growth. McKinsey & Company. https://www.m

Microsoft Azure (2023) AI-powered pricing: maximizing revenue in competitive industries. Retrieved from https://www.microsoft.com

Rieke N, Hancox J, Li W, Milletari F, Roth HR, Albarqouni S, Cardoso MJ (2020) The future of federated learning in healthcare AI. Nat Mach Intell 2(6):337–340

Yang JY (2024) Maneuver shades of pricing. In: The pricing compass. Business guides on the go. Springer, Cham. https://doi.org/10.1007/978-3-031-52060-0_5

Zhang Q, Xiong Y (2024) Harnessing AI potential in E-Commerce: improving user engagement and sales through deep learning-based product recommendations. Curr Psychol 43:30379–30401. https://doi.org/10.1007/s12144-024-06649-3

3

Case Studies: AI in Action

Introduction

AI's profound effect on pricing is manifesting itself through real-world applications across a variety of industries. From retail to hospitality, travel, and e-commerce, businesses are embracing advanced AI techniques, including Generative AI, to refine pricing strategies, improve customer satisfaction, and enhance profitability. These innovations, once confined to experimental settings, are now reshaping competitive landscapes and unlocking new sources of revenue (Bertsimas and Kallus 2020; Shankar and Bolton 2021a, b).

This chapter explores a series of compelling case studies that illustrate how AI is applied to solve specific pricing challenges. For example, dynamic pricing algorithms enable retailers to adjust their pricing in real time during flash sales, helping maintain competitiveness while preserving margins (Gans et al. 2018). Similarly, in the hospitality sector, AI helps optimize room rates, adjusting dynamically to balance occupancy and revenue during both peak and off-peak seasons (Shankar and Bolton 2021a, b). Moreover, Generative AI elevates pricing strategies by simulating scenarios, personalizing promotions, and predicting outcomes with exceptional accuracy (The Alan Turing Institute 2023).

There is a common theme across these case studies: AI is a strategic enabler. However, its effectiveness depends on more than just implementing the technology. Effective execution results from cross-functional collaboration, careful customization, and a commitment to ongoing iteration. A company's AI strategy must align with both organizational objectives and customer expectations to be truly successful (Bertsimas and Kallus 2020).

By the end of this chapter, readers will have a better understanding of AI's real-world impact on pricing strategies and a roadmap for integrating these approaches within their own businesses.[1]

Case Study 1: Ski Resort Dynamic Pricing

Background

Nestled in the scenic heart of Colorado, a mid-sized ski resort faced a challenge familiar to many others in the industry: starkly uneven demand between peak and off-peak seasons. During the winter holidays, the resort bustled with skiers eager to hit the slopes, but as soon as January rolled into February, visitor numbers plummeted. Traditional discounting tactics, such as offering flat 20% reductions during slower periods, had only limited success, if any. While a handful of locals responded to the offers, it was far from enough to compensate for the off-peak revenue shortfall. Resort management recognized the need for a more strategic, dynamic pricing approach but struggled to pinpoint how to predict and adapt to the fluctuating demand effectively.

AI Solution

The turning point came when the resort partnered with a leading AI consultancy specializing in pricing optimization. Together, they implemented a reinforcement learning (RL) algorithm, a technology well-suited for navigating dynamic and uncertain environments. This AI-powered system revamped the resort's pricing strategy by analyzing three critical inputs:

Real-time weather data:

The algorithm tapped into live forecasts to predict optimal pricing based on upcoming weather conditions. Snowstorms triggered premium pricing, while sunny skies in off-peak periods prompted subtle discounts to entice visitors.

Historical attendance trends:

Years of guest data were mined to uncover attendance patterns, such as holiday spikes or midweek dips. The algorithm used this information to forecast demand with remarkable accuracy.

---

[1] **Disclaimer:** The case studies featured in this chapter showcase real-world applications of AI in pricing across various industries. While the results and figures presented are inspired by actual trends and best practices, they do not represent proprietary data from specific companies. These examples are intended to demonstrate the potential advantages and common uses of AI-powered pricing solutions within different business contexts and should not be associated with any organization.

Competitor pricing:
The AI continuously monitored the rates of nearby ski resorts to ensure the resort's offerings remained in a competitive price corridor without sacrificing revenue.

Initially, the resort's management team was skeptical. "The very idea of handing over pricing decisions to an algorithm sounded wild," one manager admitted. However, the team quickly saw the RL system's potential. The algorithm not only adjusted pricing based on immediate factors but also adapted over time, learning from customer behavior, and refining its recommendations as patterns emerged (Talluri and van Ryzin 2004).

Outcome

The implementation of AI-enabled dynamic pricing produced amazing results. Within the first ski season, the resort experienced a 22% increase in ticket revenue, with off-season visitor numbers rising by an impressive 30%. The AI system's ability to dynamically adjust prices filled the slopes even during historically quiet periods, stabilizing revenue streams across the year.

What surprised the team most was the positive impact on customer satisfaction. Guests appreciated the transparency and fairness of the pricing model. Early planners were rewarded with discounted rates, while last-minute bookers paid a reasonable premium, a balance that resonated with diverse customer groups. One long-time visitor noted, "It finally feels like they're rewarding those of us who plan ahead without penalizing spontaneity."

The resort took the initiative further by creating AI-aided offers personalized for frequent visitors. Repeat customers received tailored loyalty discounts and bundled packages, such as ski passes paired with equipment rentals or dining credits. This approach not only deepened customer loyalty but also drove an 18% increase in repeat visits. According to the resort's marketing lead, "It was like we finally found the perfect way to thank our regulars while attracting new faces to the slopes" (Skift Insights 2023).

By embracing AI-enabled dynamic pricing, this Colorado ski resort not only revamped its revenue model but also reinvigorated its relationship with its guests. The implementation of reinforcement learning lent evidence to the power of AI to balance profitability with customer satisfaction, creating a sustainable and scalable pricing strategy that resonated with both stakeholders and visitors.

Case Study 2: Automotive Spare Parts Pricing

Background

For a global automotive supplier with a portfolio encompassing tens of thousands of spare parts, pricing was quite a piece of work. Each part came with unique demand dynamics, cost structures, competitive pressures, and varying levels of price elasticity. The company was stuck in a vicious cycle of inefficiency: underpricing parts meant losing potential revenue, while overpricing led to losing competitive bids, damaging relationships with their key clients.

"We were flying blind," admitted the senior pricing manager. The team worked with static pricing formulas and gut instinct, neither of which could adequately address the complexities of the market. Sales teams were often blindsided during negotiations, struggling to justify pricing decisions to clients. It was clear that their traditional approach was not sustainable and required an upgrade.

AI Solution

The company enlisted AI to navigate this labyrinth, implementing a gradient-boosted decision tree model tailored to their pricing challenges. This machine learning approach offered an ability to analyze massive datasets and uncover intricate patterns that would otherwise go unnoticed. The solution fulfilled three tasks:

Segmenting Parts by Price Sensitivity:

The AI segmented spare parts based on their price elasticity. High-value, specialized components with limited substitutes were assigned a pricing strategy distinct from generic parts that faced fierce competition. This segmentation allowed the company to develop nuanced pricing strategies tailored to the idiosyncrasies of each category.

Automating Bid Recommendations:

By analyzing historical data, including previous bid outcomes, competitors' pricing behaviors, and customer preferences, the AI could recommend optimal bid prices pegged to desired winning probabilities. These recommendations were tailored for specific clients, taking into account unique requirements and market conditions.

Integrating Generative AI for Negotiation Scenarios:

To complement the pricing model, the supplier introduced Generative AI tools to simulate negotiation scenarios. Sales teams could practice handling objections like, "Why should we pay this price?" or "Your competitor is offering a better deal. What's your counter?" These simulations prepared sales representatives to confidently navigate high-stakes discussions, armed with data-backed justifications.

The pricing manager reflected, "It felt like we finally had a pricing crystal ball. The recommendations seemed logical, transparent, and actionable. That transparency made all the difference."

Outcome

Within the first year, the supplier's gross margins increased by 8%, a remarkable feat in an industry where profit margins are notoriously slim. Even more impressively, win rates improved by 12%, particularly for highly elastic product categories where optimized pricing had the most significant impact.

The impact extended beyond financial metrics. Sales teams, once hesitant and reactive, became eloquent and confident in negotiations. "Instead of fumbling for answers, we could sell our pricing decisions with clarity and back them with data," a sales representative noted. This newfound confidence resonated with my clients, fostering stronger relationships and trust.

The supplier also began experimenting with bundling strategies for complementary spare parts, guided by insights from the AI model. For instance, the system discovered that bundling fast-moving items like brake pads with slow-moving components like calipers increased overall sales volumes by 15%.

As one executive summarized, "AI didn't only just fix our pricing but also fundamentally changed the way how we do business." The successful integration of advanced machine learning and Generative AI not only optimized their pricing but also elevated their operational strategy, making them more competitive and customer-centric.

Case Study 3: Retail Promotion Optimization

Background

Promotional campaigns are an essential vehicle for driving success in retail. But for one global retailer, these campaigns had started to operate more like a drain than a driver of growth. ROI was steadily declining, profit margins were eroding, and customers seemed increasingly indifferent to generic offers like "15% off everything."

"We were throwing discounts at the wall to see what stuck," admitted the head of marketing. "What we didn't realize was that not all discounts resonate equally with all customers. Worse, we were over-discounting in places where we actually didn't need to."

This blunt approach failed to excite customers miserably. At the same time, it also severely hurt the company's bottom line. It was clear that the retailer needed to rethink its promotional strategy, moving away from blanket discounts to something more targeted, precise, and profitable.

AI Solution

The company used machine learning to refine its promotional strategies. By implementing an AI-enabled model, they acquired the ability to analyze years of historical campaign data and figure out what worked best and for whom.

Performance Analysis:

The AI system dug into past promotions, identifying patterns in customer responses and isolating factors that drove conversions. For instance, it highlighted that while a 15% discount worked wonders for loyal customers, first-time buyers often responded better to free shipping offers than discounts. It also revealed areas where deep discounts led to unnecessary margin erosion, such as on already popular products or super niche products.

Segmented Strategies:

Building on the insights from the analysis, the AI model segmented customers into distinct groups, such as "high-value loyalists," "bargain hunters," and "infrequent shoppers." For each group, the system recommended tailored promotional strategies. High-value customers received exclusive discounts on premium items, while occasional shoppers were nudged with time-sensitive offers to encourage conversions.

The retailer could also personalize the marketing messages with Generative AI. Instead of generic emails, customers now received offers designed to appeal to their preferences. For example, an email to a frequent sneaker buyer might read, "Hey, Monica! Your favorite sneakers are now 20% off—just for you. Limited stock! Act fast before they're gone!"

Outcome

Targeted promotions replaced one-size-fits-all discounts, resulting in a 25% increase in promotional ROI. The retailer successfully reduced over-discounting, preserving margins while ensuring offers reached the customers most likely to respond.

On the marketing side, Generative AI brought a whole new level of personalization to customer communication. E-mail click-through rates rose by 15%, with customers responding more enthusiastically to offers that felt curated specifically for them. One customer even remarked, "It is like they actually pay attention and figure out what I want, instead of just pushing some random deals my way."

The head of marketing summed up the impact: "It is amazing how much of a difference a personal touch makes. It feels like we've finally learned how to have a proper conversation with our customers instead of shouting into the void."

Beyond immediate results, the retailer built on the momentum and devised a more sustainable promotional strategy. They could now adapt offers in real time based on customer behavior, competitive pricing, and inventory levels, ensuring they stayed ahead in a competitive market.

By embracing AI, this retailer successfully reengineered their promotional campaigns from a margin-eroding exercise into a precision-driven growth engine.

Case Study 4: Generative AI in Market Entry Pricing

Background

For a plant-based food startup, expanding into new markets offered immense potential as well as equally significant risks. Each region, from the affluent cities of Europe to the vibrant hubs of Southeast Asia, rightfully demanded its own pricing strategy. The stakes were high: overpricing would alienate new customers, while underpricing risked leaving money on the table. Traditional market research methods were slow, expensive, and often unable to capture the nuanced preferences of diverse consumer bases.

"We had to answer two questions quickly," the co-founder explained. "What are consumers willing to pay? And how does that vary from one region to another?"

AI Solution

Confronted by the complexity of regional variation, the startup implemented Generative AI to bridge the gap between data analysis and strategic pricing decisions. The advanced AI tools provided the agility and depth of insight necessary to navigate the challenges of market entry.

Willingness-to-Pay Analysis:

The AI system combed through vast quantities of unstructured data, including social media posts, customer reviews, and competitor feedback. By synthesizing these inputs, it could specify key consumer attitudes and priorities for each region. For instance, the AI revealed that customers in Western Europe were willing to pay a premium for products marketed as eco-friendly and made from locally sourced ingredients, while Southeast Asian consumers put greater emphasis on affordability and convenience.

Tailored Pricing Scenarios:

Armed with these insights, the AI generated region-specific pricing strategies. For higher-income urban areas, it suggested premium pricing tiers capitalizing on the product's unique attributes such as sustainability and health benefits. In contrast, for cost-conscious regions, it recommended smaller packaging sizes with lower price points to improve accessibility. This approach ensured pricing aligned with both economic conditions and consumer expectations.

With help of Generative AI, the startup could also simulate potential customer responses to different price points, allowing the team to assess various pricing scenarios without the need for costly pilot campaigns. "It was like running a focus group, but at the speed of light," the co-founder said.

Outcome

The first 3 months of launch saw the company's sales volumes grow 10% higher than their previous product rollouts. Revenue growth was particularly strong in urban markets where premium pricing was applied, while cost-conscious regions still delivered solid sales figures thanks to value-focused strategies.

Besides the promising financial impact, the tailored pricing approach resonated charmingly with customers. In affluent European cities, shoppers expressed appreciation for the brand's alignment with their values. In Southeast Asia, consumers welcomed the affordability and accessibility of the products. One customer remarked in an online review, "They really get what we need here: Not just a generic product, but one that fits our lifestyle and budget."

This thoughtful approach to pricing also bolstered the company's reputation as a customer-centric brand. "We didn't just roll out one-size-fits-all pricing," the co-founder noted. "It showed customers we were paying attention and that made them more willing to try our products."

By leveraging Generative AI, the startup not only mastered the complexities of regional pricing but also created a framework for future market entries. Their success proved how cutting-edge technology could turn market-specific challenges into opportunities for growth and connection.

Case Study 5: Personalizing Pricing on a Global Travel Platform

Background

For a global travel platform, loyalty was the backbone of their competitive strategy. However, despite their efforts, customers were increasingly drawn to competitors promising flashier discounts or exclusive deals. "We knew personalization was the key," shared the platform's head of customer experience. "But scaling it felt like trying to juggle millions of unique preferences while staying transparent and fair."

She addressed two common challenges in implementing personalized pricing. First, there was scalability: How could they deliver personalized pricing and promotions to millions of users without overwhelming their systems? Second, there was transparency: Tailored discounts could enhance loyalty, but any perception of arbitrariness risked alienating customers and eroding trust.

AI Solution

The platform resorted to advanced machine learning to address these challenges. The AI system analyzed customer behavior and segmented users into actionable categories based on three primary dimensions:

Travel Frequency:
Frequent travelers were rewarded with exclusive discounts, bonus loyalty points, and priority access to flash sales to enhance retention.

Preferences:
High-spending users who frequently booked luxury accommodations received offers tailored to their tastes, such as discounted premium services or upgrades. Budget-conscious travelers were nudged with value-driven offers that still upheld the platform's profitability.

Price Sensitivity:

For users highly influenced by price, the AI developed strategic discounts in a way that nudged conversions without over-discounting or eating into margins.

Building on these foundations, the platform deployed Generative AI to create real-time, personalized upsell opportunities during the checkout process. For instance, a customer booking a flight to London might see curated offers for discounted stays in four-star hotels, bundled car rentals, or premium travel insurance. These offers were designed in line with the customer's travel history and budget, ensuring they felt relevant and personalized.

The company deliberately fostered explanatory transparency for every offer. AI-enabled promotions included clear justifications such as "As a frequent traveler, you are eligible for 15% off this premium service" to reinforce trust and make the pricing personalization come across logical and fair.

Outcome

Conversion rates increased by 20% as customers engaged with tailored promotions that aligned with their preferences. Average booking value rose by 15%, driven by targeted offers that resonated with high-spending customers.

Generative AI further amplified success by enhancing upselling strategies. Through its personalized recommendations, the platform boosted ancillary revenue by an impressive 25%. Whether suggesting an upgrade to a luxury suite or a bundled car rental, the upsell offers felt thoughtful rather than intrusive.

"Customers started to feel like we really understood them," noted the customer experience lead. "Instead of generic deals, they were getting offers that made perfect sense for their travel style. That trust turned into loyalty, which turned into higher spending."

The initiative also testified to the platform's commitment to transparency. "We ensured every offer came with a clear explanation why they got it and how it benefited them," added the pricing manager. This kind of openness cultivated trust and differentiated the platform in a crowded marketplace.

By integrating machine learning with Generative AI, the travel platform achieved more than personalized pricing. It succeeded in crafting a seamless, customer-centric experience that transformed occasional users into devoted, repeat travelers.

Case Study 6: Reducing Churn for a Fitness Subscription Platform

Background

For a leading fitness subscription platform, the challenge of churn had become a big headache. Their customer engagement strategies were apparently falling short. Although the platform saw surges in sign-ups during seasonal peaks like New Year's, a considerable number of users, particularly budget-conscious ones, canceled their subscriptions within a few months. The reasons for leaving were often the same: financial constraints or dwindling motivation.

"It was so frustrating," shared the platform's retention lead. "We knew we had a great product, but clearly, we weren't doing enough to keep users engaged and loyal." Addressing the churn problem required more than standard discounts. To tackle the root cause, the platform needed a deeper understanding of customer behavior and a personalized approach to retention.

AI Solution

The platform enlisted AI in pursuit of answers, deploying machine learning models to analyze user activity, preferences, and payment behavior. The insights led to two innovative retention strategies tailored to their customers' needs:

Tailored Retention Offers:

The AI examined behavioral data to flag users who were highly engaged, i.e., those consistently streaming workout classes, achieving fitness milestones, or using premium features. For these users, the system recommended targeted offers designed to upgrade their plans. Examples included discounted premium subscriptions with personalized coaching, advanced fitness analytics, or exclusive class access. This approach encouraged already committed users to deepen their investment in the platform.

Pause-and-Resume Plans:

For at-risk customers, particularly those showing early signs of disengagement (e.g., declining workout activity or delayed payments), the AI suggested a flexible pause-and-resume feature. This option allowed users to temporarily suspend their subscriptions instead of canceling outright. Backed by research showing that flexibility can significantly enhance customer retention, this feature addressed common churn drivers like financial stress or lack of time (Cohen et al. 2021).

The retention lead explained, "The pause option was not just about preventing cancellations. We meant to prove to our users that we feel their challenges and are here to support them, even if they need a break."

Outcome

The impact was immediate and striking. Over the course of a year, churn rates dropped by 15%, marking a significant improvement for a subscription-based business. The pause-and-resume feature was particularly resonating with budget-conscious users, who appreciated the platform's customer-first approach.

Beyond reducing churn, the tailored retention offers increased the platform's average revenue per user (ARPU) by 10%. Engaged users found the premium features compelling enough to upgrade, further solidifying their loyalty.

Customer feedback reinforced the success of the strategy. One long-time subscriber shared, "I think the platform treats me like a valued customer, not just another number. The pause option came at the perfect time, and it is why I chose not to cancel right away when money got tight."

For the platform's team, the initiative was illuminating. "We're not just fighting churn anymore," the retention lead said. "We're building loyalty by showing our users that we're flexible, responsive, and genuinely invested in their success. And that's made all the difference."

Case Study 7: Real-Time Negotiation Assistance

Background

Pricing negotiations are often high-stakes moments for businesses, and for one global manufacturing firm, they felt like a recurring weak spot. Deals were delayed as sales reps grappled with pricing strategies, sometimes conceding too much to close a deal, other times holding firm and losing clients altogether.

"It was all messed up," admitted the firm's head of sales. "Some reps would give away the farm, while others would stick to their guns and scare off clients. We needed a systematic way to bring discipline to our negotiations without slowing them down."

With growing expectations for swift and well-reasoned responses, the firm sought a solution that could provide both speed and clarity.

AI Solution

The company introduced a Generative AI system specifically designed to enhance real-time negotiation support. This system addressed two critical challenges:

Generating Counter-Offers:

The AI examined historical deal data to craft counter-offers tailored to the client's specific situation. By factoring in variables such as order size, client history, market trends, and competitor pricing, the system generated offers that balanced competitiveness with profitability. The AI could instantly recommend dynamic pricing adjustments, allowing the sales team to respond to client demands without unnecessary delays.

Tailored Justifications:

In addition to recommending prices, the AI provided context-specific justifications for each counter-offer. For instance, if a client asked for a discount, the AI might reason how production costs or volume tiers factored into the price. These justifications not only enhanced client trust but also empowered sales reps to stand their ground with confidence.

The firm designed the tool to complement, not replace, human judgment. "The goal was not to take the human out of the negotiation," the sales lead explained. "It was to give our reps the tools to respond confidently and consistently, no matter the situation."

Sales reps could input details like a competitor's offer or a client's desired discount into the system. Within seconds, the AI provided a counter-proposal and supporting rationale. This allowed negotiations to flow smoothly, even under tight deadlines or intense pressure.

Outcome

The firm saw an 18% reduction in deal closure time, as sales reps no longer had to wait for approval from pricing managers or consult with other departments before responding to clients. This efficiency allowed deals to move forward faster, which was appreciated by clients who valued timely and well-justified proposals. Additionally, the consistency in the AI's recommendations led to an 8% improvement in margins on negotiated contracts, as pricing was now more closely aligned with both market trends and the firm's financial goals.

But the most momentous change occurred within the sales team itself. Initially, there was skepticism about the role of AI in the negotiation process. Over time, however, sales reps began to appreciate the tool, feeling empowered rather than replaced. "The robot does not replace our instincts; it is making us better, sharper, faster, and more confident in the room," one rep explained. This confidence, supported by data-driven insights, improved the team's ability to handle objections and made them feel more in control during negotiations.

Positive client feedback corroborated the success of the initiative. One client commented, "It was refreshing to see a supplier that could justify their pricing in such a systematic way. The entire process suddenly feels much more collaborative and trustworthy." This shift in how the firm approached pricing discussions helped build stronger, trust-based relationships with clients, turning what was once a source of tension into a competitive advantage. By blending the analytical power of Generative AI with the know-how and judgment of the sales team, the firm was able to streamline its negotiation process, close deals more efficiently, and improve profitability, all while bolstering customer loyalty.

Behind the Curtains: AI Algorithm Codes

To bring the preceding case studies to life, we should take a look behind the scenes at the AI algorithms that make them possible. This section provides simplified code examples that illustrate how you can implement similar solutions using Python. Each snippet aligns with one of the cases, offering a practical glimpse into how AI can be applied to real-world pricing and business challenges.

These examples focus on clarity and accessibility, using popular Python libraries like scikit-learn for machine learning, TensorFlow for deep learning, and Prophet for time-series forecasting. Whether you are a data scientist, a business leader, or simply curious about the mechanics of AI, this section is designed to offer concrete insights into how these tools work in practice.

Now let's dive into the code that powers AI-enabled pricing and discover how these algorithms can translate data into actionable strategies.

Algorithm for Case Study 1: Ski Resort Dynamic Pricing

AI Algorithm: Q-learning for dynamic pricing.

```python
import numpy as np
import random

# Define the environment
states = {'low_demand': 0, 'high_demand': 1}
actions = {'price_low': 0, 'price_medium': 1, 'price_high': 2}
rewards = {
    'low_demand': {'price_low': 10, 'price_medium': 5, 'price_high': 1},
    'high_demand': {'price_low': -10, 'price_medium': 5, 'price_high': 20}
}

# Initialize Q-table
q_table = np.zeros((len(states), len(actions)))

# Parameters
learning_rate = 0.1
discount_factor = 0.9
epsilon = 1.0  # Initial exploration rate
epsilon_decay = 0.995  # Decay rate per episode
epsilon_min = 0.01
episodes = 5000

# Function to choose action (epsilon-greedy)
def choose_action(state_index):
    if random.uniform(0, 1) < epsilon: #Exploration
        return random.choice(range(len(actions)))
    return np.argmax(q_table[state_index]) #Exploitation

# Simulate environment
for episode in range(episodes):
    state_index = random.choice(list(states.values()))
    # Start with a random state
    done = False
    step = 0
```

```
while not done:
    action_index = choose_action(state_index)
    action = list(actions.keys())[action_index]
    reward = rewards[list(states.keys())[state_index]]
    [action]

    # More realistic state transition (probability-based)
    if state_index == states['low_demand']:
        next_state_index = np.random.choice([states['low_
            demand'], states['high_demand']], p=[0.8, 0.2])
    else:
        next_state_index = np.random.choice([states['low_
            demand'], states['high_demand']], p=[0.3, 0.7])

    # Q-learning update rule
    q_table[state_index, action_index] =
    (1 - learning_rate) * q_table[state_index, action_
    index] + \ learning_rate * (reward + discount_factor
    * np.max(q_table[next_state_index]))

    state_index = next_state_index
    step+= 1

    # Limit steps per episode to prevent infinite loops
    if step>= 10:
        done = True

# Decay epsilon
epsilon = max(epsilon * epsilon_decay, epsilon_min)

# Display final Q-table
print("Learned Q-table:")
print(q_table)
```

Explanation:

In this simplified Q-learning algorithm, the ski resort dynamically adjusts prices based on demand states. The model learns over time which pricing action leads to the highest reward (revenue) for each demand state.

Algorithm for Case Study 2: Automotive Spare Parts Pricing

AI Algorithm: Gradient Boosting for predictive pricing.

```python
import pandas as pd
import numpy as np
from sklearn.ensemble import GradientBoostingRegressor
from sklearn.model_selection import train_test_split, GridSearchCV
from sklearn.metrics import mean_absolute_error, r2_score
from sklearn.preprocessing import StandardScaler

# Simulate a larger dataset (50 samples)
np.random.seed(42)
data_size = 50
data = pd.DataFrame({
    'part_cost': np.random.uniform(100, 300, data_size),
    'demand': np.random.uniform(50, 350, data_size),
    'competitor_price': np.random.uniform(100, 320, data_size),
})

# Target variable (price) is simulated based on a pricing rule with noise
data['price'] = 1.2 * data['part_cost'] + 0.5 * data['demand'] + 0.8 * data['competitor_price'] + np.random.normal(0, 10, data_size)

# Features & target
X = data[['part_cost', 'demand', 'competitor_price']]
y = data['price']

# Train-test split
X_train, X_test, y_train, y_test = train_test_split(X, y, test_size=0.2, random_state=42)

# Feature scaling (optional, for improved training stability)
scaler = StandardScaler()
X_train_scaled = scaler.fit_transform(X_train)
X_test_scaled = scaler.transform(X_test)

# Hyperparameter tuning using GridSearchCV
param_grid = {
```

```
    'n_estimators': [100, 200],
    'learning_rate': [0.05, 0.1],
    'max_depth': [3, 5]
}

grid_search = GridSearchCV(GradientBoostingRegressor(),
param_grid, cv=3, scoring='neg_mean_absolute_error')
grid_search.fit(X_train_scaled, y_train)

# Train model with best parameters
best_model = grid_search.best_estimator_
best_model.fit(X_train_scaled, y_train)

# Predict prices
predicted_prices = best_model.predict(X_test_scaled)

# Evaluate performance
mae = mean_absolute_error(y_test, predicted_prices)
r2 = r2_score(y_test, predicted_prices)

print(f"Best Model: {grid_search.best_params_}")
print(f"Mean Absolute Error: {mae:.2f}")
print(f"R² Score: {r2:.2f}")
print("Predicted Prices:", predicted_prices)
```

Explanation:
This code exemplifies how to use Gradient Boosting to predict optimal prices for automotive spare parts based on factors like part cost, demand, and competitor pricing.

Algorithm for Case Study 3: Retail Promotion Optimization

AI Algorithm: Random Forest for promotion optimization.

```
import pandas as pd
import numpy as np
from sklearn.ensemble import RandomForestRegressor
from sklearn.model_selection import train_test_split, GridSearchCV
from sklearn.metrics import mean_absolute_error, r2_score
from sklearn.preprocessing import OneHotEncoder

# Simulate a larger dataset (50 samples)
```

```python
np.random.seed(42)
data_size = 50
data = pd.DataFrame({
    'previous_sales': np.random.randint(1000, 2000,
    data_size),
    'discount_percentage': np.random.randint(5, 30,
    data_size),
    'promotion_type': np.random.choice(['Sale', 'Flash Sale',
    'Bundle'], data_size)
})

# Encode categorical variable 'promotion_type'
encoder = OneHotEncoder(sparse=False, drop='first')  # One-Hot
Encoding
encoded_promo = encoder.fit_transform(data[['promotion_type']])
encoded_promo_df = pd.DataFrame(encoded_promo,
columns=encoder.get_feature_names_out())

# Add encoded promotion type back into dataset
data = pd.concat([data, encoded_promo_df], axis=1)
data.drop(columns=['promotion_type'], inplace=True)

# Target variable (sales after promotion) simulated with
some noise
data['sales_after_promotion'] = (
    data['previous_sales'] * (1 + data['discount_percentage']
    / 100) +
    100 * encoded_promo_df.sum(axis=1) +  # Promotion type effect
    np.random.normal(0, 50, data_size)  # Random noise
)

# Features & target
X = data.drop(columns=['sales_after_promotion'])
y = data['sales_after_promotion']

# Train-test split
X_train, X_test, y_train, y_test = train_test_split(X, y,
test_size=0.2, random_state=42)

# Hyperparameter tuning with GridSearchCV
param_grid = {
    'n_estimators': [100, 200],
    'max_depth': [3, 5, 7],
    'min_samples_split': [2, 5]
}
```

```python
grid_search = GridSearchCV(RandomForestRegressor(), param_
grid, cv=3, scoring='neg_mean_absolute_error')
grid_search.fit(X_train, y_train)

# Train best model
best_model = grid_search.best_estimator_
best_model.fit(X_train, y_train)

# Predict & evaluate
predicted_sales = best_model.predict(X_test)
mae = mean_absolute_error(y_test, predicted_sales)
r2 = r2_score(y_test, predicted_sales)

print(f"Best Model Parameters: {grid_search.best_params_}")
print(f"Mean Absolute Error: {mae:.2f}")
print(f"R² Score: {r2:.2f}")
print("Predicted Sales After Promotion:", predicted_sales)
```

Explanation:
Random Forests are used here to predict how sales will change after running promotions based on past sales, discount percentage, and promotion type.

Algorithm for Case Study 4: Generative AI in Market Entry Pricing

AI Algorithm: Generative Pre-trained Transformer (GPT-4) for scenario generation.

```python
import openai
import os
import time

# Load API key from environment variable (avoid hardcoding
for security)
openai.api_key = os.getenv("OPENAI_API_KEY")  # Ensure you
set this variable in your environment

# Function to generate a pricing scenario with error handling
and retries
def generate_pricing_scenario(prompt, model="gpt-4",
max_retries=3):
    attempt = 0
```

```python
    while attempt < max_retries:
        try:
            response = openai.ChatCompletion.create(
                model=model,
                messages=[
                    {"role": "system", "content": "You are an
                    expert in pricing strategies."},
                    {"role": "user", "content": prompt}
                ],
                max_tokens=500, #Increased limit for better
                responses
                temperature=0.7
            )
            generated_scenario = response.get("choices",
            [{}])[0].get("message", {}).get("content",
            "").strip()
            
            if not generated_scenario:
                raise ValueError("Received an empty response
                from GPT-4.")
            
            return generated_scenario
        
        except Exception as e:
            print(f"Attempt {attempt + 1} failed: {e}")
            attempt += 1
            time.sleep(2)   # Wait before retrying
    
    return "Error: Unable to generate a pricing scenario
    after multiple attempts."

# Allow user input for customization
user_prompt = input("Enter your scenario prompt (or press
Enter to use the default): ").strip()
if not user_prompt:
    user_prompt = """
    Generate a pricing strategy for launching a plant-based
    product in the European market,
    considering local economic conditions and competitor
    pricing.
    """

# Generate and display the scenario
pricing_scenario = generate_pricing_scenario(user_prompt)
print("\nGenerated Pricing Scenario:\n", pricing_scenario)
```

Explanation:
Generative AI can be utilized to simulate pricing scenarios based on the characteristics of local business environments, allowing businesses to generate tailored pricing strategies for market entry.

Algorithm for Case Study 5: Personalizing Pricing on a Global Travel Platform

AI Algorithm: K-Means Clustering for customer segmentation.

```
import pandas as pd
import numpy as np
import matplotlib.pyplot as plt
from sklearn.cluster import KMeans
from sklearn.preprocessing import StandardScaler
from yellowbrick.cluster import KElbowVisualizer

# Simulate travel data
data = pd.DataFrame({
    'customer_id': [1, 2, 3, 4, 5, 6, 7, 8, 9, 10],
    'travel_frequency': [5, 10, 3, 12, 6, 9, 15, 4, 7, 8],
    'price_sensitivity': [0.8, 0.6, 0.9, 0.5, 0.7, 0.8, 0.4,
        0.7, 0.6, 0.5]
})

X = data[['travel_frequency', 'price_sensitivity']]

# Standardize the features for better clustering performance
scaler = StandardScaler()
X_scaled = scaler.fit_transform(X)

# Use Elbow Method to find optimal number of clusters
model = KMeans(init='k-means++', random_state=42)
visualizer = KElbowVisualizer(model, k=(2,6))   # Test between 2 to 6 clusters
visualizer.fit(X_scaled)
visualizer.show()

# Choose the optimal k from the Elbow method
optimal_k = visualizer.elbow_value_
```

```
# Apply K-Means with optimal number of clusters
kmeans = KMeans(n_clusters=optimal_k, init='k-means++',
random_state=42)
data['customer_segment'] = kmeans.fit_predict(X_scaled)

# Visualize clusters
plt.figure(figsize=(8,6))
plt.scatter(data['travel_frequency'], data['price_
sensitivity'], c=data['customer_segment'], cmap='viridis',
edgecolors='k')
plt.xlabel('Travel Frequency')
plt.ylabel('Price Sensitivity')
plt.title(f'Customer Segmentation (k={optimal_k})')
plt.colorbar(label='Cluster')
plt.grid(True)
plt.show()
```

Explanation:
K-Means clustering is applied to segment customers based on their travel frequency and price sensitivity. By standardizing features and using the Elbow Method to determine the optimal number of clusters, the model ensures accurate segmentation.

Algorithm for Case Study 6: Reducing Churn for a Fitness Subscription Platform

AI Algorithm: Decision Tree for retention strategy prediction.

```
import pandas as pd
from sklearn.tree import DecisionTreeClassifier, plot_tree
from sklearn.model_selection import train_test_split,
cross_val_score
from sklearn.metrics import accuracy_score, precision_score,
recall_score, f1_score

# Simulate subscription data (e.g., usage frequency,
engagement, subscription type)
data = pd.DataFrame({
    'usage_frequency': [5, 2, 8, 3, 6, 7, 4, 9, 1, 5],
    'engagement_score': [90, 45, 85, 50, 65, 75, 55, 95, 30, 60],
    'churned': [0, 1, 0, 1, 0, 0, 1, 0, 1, 0]  # 1: Churned,
    0: Retained
})
```

```python
X = data[['usage_frequency', 'engagement_score']]
y = data['churned']

# Split data into train and test sets
X_train, X_test, y_train, y_test = train_test_split(X, y,
test_size=0.2, random_state=42)

# Train Decision Tree model
model = DecisionTreeClassifier(max_depth=3, random_state=42)
model.fit(X_train, y_train)

# Predict churn for test data
predicted_churn = model.predict(X_test)

# Evaluate model performance
accuracy = accuracy_score(y_test, predicted_churn)
precision = precision_score(y_test, predicted_churn)
recall = recall_score(y_test, predicted_churn)
f1 = f1_score(y_test, predicted_churn)

# Print metrics
print("Predicted churn:", predicted_churn)
print(f"Accuracy: {accuracy:.4f}")
print(f"Precision: {precision:.4f}")
print(f"Recall: {recall:.4f}")
print(f"F1 Score: {f1:.4f}")

# Visualize the Decision Tree
plt.figure(figsize=(12, 8))
plot_tree(model, filled=True, feature_names=X.columns, class_names=['Retained', 'Churned'], rounded=True)
plt.title('Decision Tree for Churn Prediction')
plt.show()
```

Explanation:
Decision Trees are adopted to predict whether a user is likely to churn based on their usage frequency and engagement score, informing retention strategies. The model's performance is evaluated using metrics like accuracy, precision, recall, and F1 score.

Algorithm for Case Study 7: Real-Time Negotiation Assistance

AI Algorithm: Generative Pre-trained Transformer (GPT-4) for real-time counter-offer generation during negotiations.

```
import openai
import os

# Securely fetch OpenAI API key from environment variable
openai.api_key = os.getenv("OPENAI_API_KEY")

# Example input data: contract terms, customer profile,
competitor offers
customer_profile = "Customer: ABC Corp, industry:
Manufacturing, negotiation history: prefers long-term
contracts, current contract volume: 1000 units"
competitor_offer = "Competitor Price: $500 per unit, 12-month
contract, no discount"

# Additional context for a more tailored counter-offer
unique_selling_points = "Our product offers superior quality
and faster delivery times, which have been valued by similar
customers in your industry."

# Combine all relevant data into a comprehensive prompt
prompt = f"""
Generate a counter-offer based on the following data:
Customer Profile: {customer_profile}
Competitor's Offer: {competitor_offer}
Our pricing strategy: Flexible pricing with a discount on
long-term contracts.
Unique Selling Points: {unique_selling_points}
Our business constraints: Maximum discount of 10%, contract
length: 12-24 months.
"""

# Use OpenAI's GPT-4 model to generate the counter-offer
response = openai.Completion.create(
    model="gpt-4",
    prompt=prompt,
    max_tokens=250,
    temperature=0.6,  # Lower temperature for more consistent
    responses
```

```
        top_p=1.0,
        n=1,
        stop=["\n"]
    )

    # Extract and display the generated counter-offer
    generated_text = response.choices[0].text.strip()

    # Ensure the counter-offer aligns with business constraints
    (e.g., max discount, contract length)
    if "discount" in generated_text and "long-term contract" in
    generated_text:
        print("Generated Counter-Offer:", generated_text)
    else:
        print("Counter-offer not aligned with business
        constraints. Please review manually.")
```

Explanation:
In this case study, the Generative AI model, GPT-4, generates a real-time counter-offer during negotiations. The input includes the customer's profile, the competitor's offer, and the pricing strategy. The model uses this information to craft a tailored counter-offer that helps sales teams dynamically respond during negotiations with better-informed proposals.

Lessons from the Trenches

The growing ensemble of AI models act together in complementary ways to enhance pricing strategies. While AI technologies, like machine learning, excel at analytics, managing pricing with accuracy, by analyzing data patterns, forecasting demand, and setting prices accordingly, Generative AI adds an extra dimension of creativity and flexibility. Machine learning helps refine pricing models based on data, whereas Generative AI takes that data further by generating customized pricing scenarios and personalized offers that cater to different customer segments (Zhou 2023a, b). For instance, while machine learning may adjust prices based on demand fluctuations, Generative AI can craft tailored discounts or bundles for individual customers, taking into account their purchasing history and preferences.

Effective data integration plays a decisive role for successful AI deployment. It is not just about having access to vast amounts of data. Instead, it is pivotal to organize and structure the big data in ways that AI systems can process efficiently. In the travel and transportation industries, for example, real-time data integration is critical for AI systems to adjust prices dynamically in response to changes in supply and demand. Uber, for instance, uses data streams from both drivers and passengers to update fares during peak times (Zhou 2023a, b). Without the ability to seamlessly integrate data from various sources, AI models would not be able to provide timely and accurate pricing recommendations.

The return on investment (ROI) from AI-enabled pricing typically becomes evident within a matter of months after implementation. For example, companies in the retail and hospitality industries that implement AI pricing strategies often see significant revenue improvements within the first 6 months. Retailers that use AI for dynamic pricing can adjust prices in real time, boosting revenue during periods of high demand (Zhou 2023a, b). By continuously learning from customer behavior, demand fluctuations, and market trends, AI solutions refine their pricing strategies over time. This results in both short-term revenue increases and stronger, more trusting relationships with customers, as personalized and fair pricing models based on actual demand replace static pricing formulas.

References

Bertsimas D, Kallus N (2020) Machine learning for dynamic pricing. Manag Sci 66(3):825–842. https://doi.org/10.1287/mnsc.2019.3257

Cohen M, Lobel I, Perakis G (2021) Dynamic customer retention strategies: Evidence from AI-enabled models. J AI Res 70:231–249. https://doi.org/10.1613/jair.2021

Gans JS, Goldfarb A, Agrawal A (2018) Prediction machines: the simple economics of artificial intelligence. Harvard Business Review Press

Shankar V, Bolton RN (2021a) AI and pricing: advances, opportunities, and challenges. J Mark Res 58(2):367–385. https://doi.org/10.1177/0022243720972364

Shankar V, Bolton RN (2021b) AI and customer retention: strategies for success. J Mark Res 58(2):367–385. https://doi.org/10.1177/0022243720972364

Skift Insights. (2023). AI-enabled strategies in travel and hospitality: The dynamic pricing advantage. Retrieved from https://www.skift.com

Talluri KT, van Ryzin GJ (2004) The theory and practice of revenue management. Springer

The Alan Turing Institute. (2023). Generative AI for consumer insights and market analysis. Retrieved from https://www.turing.ac.uk

Zhou J (2023a) Leveraging AI for dynamic pricing in the digital economy. J Artif Intell Bus 19(2):34–48

Zhou X (2023b) The impact of dynamic pricing in retail: How AI is changing the game. J Retail Technol 35(4):48–60

4

Guiding Organizational Change for AI-Enabled Pricing

Introduction

AI-enabled pricing embodies a deep organizational transformation. It is the turning point where traditional pricing methods, rooted in intuition and spreadsheets, metamorphose into AI-powered systems that deliver precision, agility, and enhanced decision-making. This transition offers unprecedented opportunities but also poses significant challenges (Brynjolfsson and McAfee 2014; Davenport and Ronanki 2018).

The idea of leveraging AI to drive pricing decisions often elicits mixed reactions. Leadership may be excited about AI's potential to boost revenue and build competitive advantages. However, various hurdles abound, e.g., persuading skeptical stakeholders, addressing resistance among teams accustomed to manual methods, and ensuring that AI systems uphold fairness, ethics, and organizational values. For instance, studies show that resistance from employees often stems from a fear of losing control over decision-making processes or a lack of trust in AI-enabled recommendations (McKinsey & Company 2023).

Building on the AI implementation process discussed in Chap. 2, this chapter delves into the leadership dimension, specifically, how leaders can effectively navigate these challenges. It provides insights into crafting compelling arguments for AI adoption, strategies to engage resistant teams, and frameworks for addressing the cultural and ethical complexities inherent in deploying AI solutions (Davenport and Ronanki 2018).

Case studies throughout the chapter illustrate these challenges and successes. For example, some companies have successfully involved sales teams in the development phase of AI-powered pricing models, transforming skeptics into advocates by showing how their expertise enhances the system's recommendations. Similarly, transparency in AI operations has proven to foster trust among internal stakeholders and customers alike, a crucial factor in AI adoption (The Alan Turing Institute 2023).

In guiding your organization through this exciting process, you will not only implement AI but also reimagine the role of pricing as a strategic, customer-focused function. While AI may drive the algorithms, it is visionary leaders who inspire teams to embrace change and realize the full potential of innovation.

Making the Case for AI in Pricing

Picture yourself addressing your organization's leadership team, tasked with presenting the transformative possibilities of AI in pricing. The atmosphere is a mix of intrigue and doubt, and your goal is clear: this is not just another pitch for adopting a new technology; it comes down to articulating why AI in pricing is essential for achieving the company's strategic goals and staying competitive in today's fast-changing markets (Brynjolfsson and McAfee 2014; Davenport and Ronanki 2018).

Effectively making this case requires a blend of storytelling, analytical rigor, and strategic alignment. You need to address the concerns of diverse stakeholders, be it the CFO focused on budgetary implications or the sales director seeking innovative ways to increase revenue. At the core of your argument should be unambiguous evidence of how AI-enabled pricing delivers measurable results, from revenue growth to improved operational efficiency (Smith and Anderson 2021).

Communicating the Value of AI to Stakeholders

At the heart of your presentation lies the value proposition: Why is investing in AI pricing solutions not just advantageous but critical? Let's consider the example of Vanessa, a global pricing manager at a large electronics distributor. For years, her team relied on manual processes to set prices across thousands of SKUs, resulting in frequent errors and missed opportunities. Customers often negotiated steep discounts that eroded margins, while competitors outpaced them with more agile pricing strategies (Smith et al. 2022).

When Vanessa proposed implementing AI for dynamic pricing, initial reactions were mixed. The COO was enthusiastic, but the CFO hesitated, citing concerns about cost. Acknowledging these reservations, Vanessa crafted her pitch with precision. She began by outlining the tangible benefits:

1. **Revenue Growth**: Vanessa emphasized how AI enables real-time pricing adjustments based on demand, competitor actions, and customer willingness to pay. She referenced studies showing that even a 1% improvement in price optimization could result in an 8–10% increase in operating profit (Brynjolfsson and McAfee 2014; Gans et al. 2018).
2. **Competitive Edge**: Vanessa positioned AI as a strategic necessity, noting that the leading companies in the industry had already implemented similar solutions. Falling behind could risk market share and customer loyalty. She cited a case study where predictive pricing models allowed a rival company to reduce discounting frequency by 20% while upkeeping customer satisfaction (Davenport and Ronanki 2018).
3. **Operational Efficiency**: She emphasized how AI could alleviate her team's manual workload, reducing errors, streamlining processes, and enabling them to focus on strategic tasks like identifying emerging market trends.
4. **Cost Savings:** By automating routine operations, the team could achieve significant cost savings through improved accuracy, faster turnaround times, and reduced reliance on external resources.

To further substantiate her argument, Vanessa shared examples of companies in similar situations that had successfully implemented AI pricing systems. One competitor, for example, achieved significant revenue gains by integrating predictive models that optimized discounting strategies while preserving customer loyalty (Shankar and Bolton 2021).

Vanessa's data-driven approach clicked with the leadership team. By aligning AI's capabilities with the organization's strategic goals and addressing specific stakeholder concerns, she successfully made a case that adopting AI pricing solutions was not just a technological upgrade but a crucial investment in the company's future.

Aligning AI-Enabled Pricing with Broader Business Goals

The success of any AI-enabled pricing solution depends on its alignment with the organization's overarching objectives. AI is not just another analytical tool;

it is a strategic enabler that connects pricing optimization with outcomes that matter most to the business (Davenport and Ronanki 2018).

Consider the experience of a global retail chain navigating this dynamic. The CIO had touted AI pricing for months but struggled to gain buy-in from the CEO, who was singularly fixated on improving customer satisfaction metrics. "Customer loyalty is non-negotiable," the CEO often emphasized. "If we lose their trust, they'll go elsewhere."

The turning point occurred when the CIO reframed the proposal to center on customer satisfaction. Instead of positioning AI as a cost-optimization tool, the CIO highlighted its potential for delivering personalized, fair pricing. He presented case studies illustrating how machine learning models could distinguish customers at risk of churning and provide targeted incentives to retain them.

"AI is not all about improving margins," he explained. "It allows us to create pricing experiences that resonate with our customers, offering discounts that feel personalized and building trust through fairness." By aligning the proposal with the CEO's goals, the conversation shifted. The CEO, previously unconvinced, approved the initiative the following month, recognizing its potential to enhance both loyalty and profitability (Smith and Anderson 2021).

For AI-enabled pricing to succeed, it must integrate seamlessly with the company's mission. Whether the focus is customer retention, revenue growth, or competitive differentiation, aligning the technology with core business goals transforms it from a tool into a transformative strategy.

Crafting a Compelling Narrative

While data and metrics form the backbone of any business proposal, storytelling has the unique power to create emotional connections and highlight the human side of challenges and opportunities. A well-told story can make your case for AI in pricing resonate far more deeply with your audience.

Consider the example of a revenue manager at a regional airline. Instead of diving directly into numbers, he began his presentation by recounting a vivid personal experience. During a sudden snowstorm, his team struggled to manually adjust ticket prices in real time. Competitors swiftly undercut them to capitalize on demand, while his airline lagged behind, leading to both revenue loss and frustrated customers. "That day was a wake-up call," he reflected. "The market moves faster than we can react manually, and we can't afford to let that happen again."

This story not only captured attention but also humanized the problem. He then seamlessly connected this experience to how AI could provide a solution. Predictive analytics, he explained, would allow the airline to foresee demand surges in similar scenarios, dynamically adjusting prices to stay competitive while safeguarding profit margins. His narrative struck a chord because it was relatable, highlighting a pain point that most of the audience in the room had experienced.

By linking the technology to real-world struggles and aspirations, he made the case for AI pricing compelling and memorable. This storytelling approach underscores how AI is not just about algorithms; it is about solving the practical challenges that businesses face daily (Chui et al. 2021; Davenport and Ronanki 2018).

Addressing Common Concerns

Successfully advocating for AI-enabled pricing requires proactively detecting and addressing potential objections from stakeholders. Common concerns often revolve around costs, complexity, and potential disruption to existing workflows. By openly acknowledging these issues and providing clear, evidence-based solutions, you can build confidence and support for your initiative.

Take the example of a manufacturing firm where leadership hesitated to adopt AI pricing due to cost concerns. The pricing lead addressed the issue directly: "Yes, there's an upfront investment," she acknowledged, "but let's look at the payback period." She presented a financial model predicting that the solution would achieve breakeven within 12 months and continue generating substantial returns over the long term. By quantifying the ROI, she reframed the cost as an investment rather than an expense, easing financial concerns (Binns 2018; Choudhury et al. 2022).

For stakeholders apprehensive about complexity, the focus shifted to simplicity. "You do not need to understand every algorithm," she reassured the team. "Think of this system like a GPS for pricing. It does the complex calculations in the background and provides you with clear, actionable directions." By emphasizing intuitive interfaces and actionable insights, she highlighted how AI could simplify decision-making rather than complicate it (Lee 2019; Kumar and Shah 2021).

This approach accentuates the value of transparency and relatability in overcoming objections. Addressing concerns head-on with tangible examples and practical analogies helps demystify AI, fostering trust and alignment across teams.

The Cardinal Message

Making a compelling case for AI in pricing requires convincing key stakeholders how these capabilities align with your organization's unique challenges, objectives, and values. The conversation should center on what resonates most with your stakeholders, whether it is driving cost efficiency, enhancing customer loyalty, or securing a competitive advantage. Tailoring your message to these priorities ensures that you connect with their concerns and aspirations (Chui et al. 2021; Hagel 2020).

The most persuasive arguments do not center around data and algorithms; they must have to do with transformation. The most impactful narratives show how AI can solve pressing problems, unlock new opportunities, and eventually lead to meaningful organizational growth. The AI story becomes compelling not when you emphasize the technical sophistication of the algorithms, but when you show how they reduced customer churn and increased revenue by tailoring offers to customer preferences (Kumar and Shah 2021; Lee 2019).

As you prepare your case, think of yourself as more than just an advocate for AI: you are a storyteller. Your role is to craft a vision of how AI can revolutionize operations, improve outcomes, and guide the organization toward its goals. A strong narrative not only captures attention but also inspires action, paving the way for the successful integration of AI-enabled pricing across the business (Mikalef et al. 2019; Smith and Anderson 2021).

Navigating Challenges

Incorporating AI into pricing is akin to embarking on a journey through uncharted territory. While the potential gains such as improved profitability and data-driven decision-making are enticing, the process is seldom straightforward. Organizations frequently encounter technical hurdles, such as integrating AI into existing systems, as well as cultural resistance from employees reluctant to embrace innovative technologies. However, these challenges, while seemingly formidable, offer unique opportunities to refine strategies, foster collaboration, and build a robust foundation for long-term success (Mikalef et al. 2019; Chui et al. 2021).

Rather than perceiving objections as roadblocks, it is more constructive to approach them as steppingstones. Overcoming these issues requires strategic planning, open communication, and adaptability. By addressing resistance and aligning cross-functional teams, organizations can unlock AI's transformative potential and secure a competitive edge in today's rapidly changing markets (Hagel 2020).

Addressing Resistance to Change

Resistance to change is an enduring challenge in any organizational transition. Employees often perceive AI systems as a threat to their roles, expertise, or long-standing processes. Effective adoption of AI demands empathy, transparency, and tangible demonstrations of the technology's value.

Consider the example of a mid-sized manufacturing company that sought to deploy AI pricing to streamline its quoting process. The sales team, accustomed to "old-school" negotiations, initially opposed the idea, fearing that algorithms would diminish their relationships with clients. "If customers believe we're just relying on machines for pricing, they'll take their business elsewhere," one senior salesperson argued.

Recognizing these concerns, leadership opted for a collaborative approach. They involved the sales team in a pilot program, allowing them to explore how AI could complement their experience and ability. The AI system analyzed historical data and competitor benchmarks to recommend pricing tiers in real time. Sales representatives retained the ability to override suggestions, which helped ease apprehensions about losing autonomy.

One salesperson noted a breakthrough during the trial: "At first, I doubted its effectiveness. But when the system recommended a higher price for a customer I expected to negotiate aggressively, and they accepted it, I realized I had been undervaluing our products."

This pivotal moment marked a shift in perception. The sales team began to view AI not as a replacement but as a decision-support tool that enhanced their efficiency and confidence. Within 6 months, the company rolled out the AI solution company-wide, with sales representatives emerging as its strongest advocates (Hagel 2020; Davenport and Ronanki 2018).

Tackling Data Silos and Technical Challenges

Even the most motivated teams can encounter technical roadblocks that hinder the successful implementation of AI-enabled pricing strategies. A particularly pervasive issue is data silos. Separate systems and departmental silos prevent the aggregation of critical information, hindering effective AI model training (Chen et al. 2021). Without consistent and integrated data, AI algorithms may yield inconsistent or misleading results, undermining decision-making processes.

A major retail chain offers a compelling example of this challenge. When the company initially tried to deploy AI-powered pricing, the models produced erratic outcomes. The root cause being datasets scattered across different systems. Sales data was stored in one platform, inventory records in another, and customer behavior metrics in yet another.

Recognizing the critical need for data harmonization, the company assembled a cross-functional task force with members from sales, IT, and supply chain teams. Their mission was to integrate all relevant datasets into a centralized cloud platform as a single source of truth, ensuring uniformity and compatibility. The process involved cleaning, standardizing, and unifying the data, a project that took a painful year to complete.

However, once the integration was finalized, the outcome was more satisfying. The AI model began generating reliable insights, such as identifying overstocked items suitable for markdowns and pinpointing underpriced products with hidden profit potential. The effectiveness of AI pricing systems hinges not only on the sophistication of the algorithms but also on the robustness of the underlying data infrastructure (Chen et al. 2021).

Managing Immediate Gains While Pursuing Long-Term Goals

A critical challenge when implementing AI-enabled pricing is striking a balance between the immediate need for visible returns and the broader strategic vision that unfolds over time. Stakeholders are often more keen about short-term outcomes, like an immediate increase in margins or revenue, but the true strength of AI lies in its ability to learn, adapt, and deliver compounded value in the long run (Bertsimas and Kallus 2020; Choi et al. 2021).

For instance, a regional grocery chain faced this exact dilemma when rolling out its AI pricing solution. Leadership emphasized rapid ROI, expecting significant margin improvements right from the outset. However, early results were underwhelming as the AI system required time to learn from sales data, customer behavior, and market dynamics.

The pricing team faced growing pressure from stakeholders who were eager to justify the investment. "It is hard to convince the leadership that AI is a long-term strategy, not a quick fix," the head of pricing shared during internal discussions.

To address this, the implementation team adopted a two-pronged approach. They targeted "quick wins" by fine-tuning prices for high-margin products consistently undervalued in their portfolio. Concurrently, they educated stakeholders on the gradual yet profound impact of AI in the long run, highlighting how predictive analytics would master the pricing strategy for thousands of products.

Over 6 months, the system began yielding stable results: a 3% increase in gross margins and a 10% reduction in markdown waste. Leadership recognized the benefits of balancing short-term actions with long-term vision, and the initiative became a success story in strategic AI adoption. The grocery chain's experience underscores the importance of aligning short-term achievements with sustained investment in AI capabilities (Chen et al. 2021; Choudhury et al. 2022).

The Human Factor: Connecting Teams and Technology

While technological challenges in AI adoption often dominate the conversation, the human factor is equally critical. Collaboration among data scientists, IT specialists, pricing managers, and frontline employees is essential to ensure that AI systems deliver practical, actionable insights.

A B2B hardware supplier exemplifies this dynamic. Eager to leverage AI pricing to outmaneuver larger competitors, the company initially faced obstacles aligning its technical and business teams. The data science team developed an advanced pricing algorithm, but the sales team found the recommendations impractical. "The system might make sense theoretically," one salesperson remarked, "but it didn't match the realities of what our customers were willing to pay."

To bridge this gap, the hardware supplier facilitated cross-functional workshops. These sessions brought together sales representatives and data scientists to refine the algorithm collaboratively. Sales reps shared insights on customer price sensitivities across different segments, while data scientists integrated these real-world nuances into the model.

This partnership yielded remarkable results. Within a year, the company achieved a 7% improvement in win rates on competitive bids. Beyond the measurable gains, the process fostered trust and stronger communication between teams, paving the way for future AI projects (Mikalef et al. 2019; Heaton 2017).

Lessons Learned

Effectively tackling the challenges of AI-enabled pricing requires a combination of technical prowess and a human-centered approach. Organizations that succeed are not those that sidestep obstacles but those that confront them with a mindset of learning, cooperation, and adaptability.

Empathy Drives Success: Engage with your teams to understand their concerns, ensuring they feel included in the process. AI solutions thrive when perceived as collaborative tools rather than replacements for human expertise (Davenport and Ronanki 2018).

Data Infrastructure is Foundational: Unified, high-quality data is critical to AI's success. Prioritize cleaning and organizing datasets, even if it requires considerable time and resources (Heaton 2017; Choi et al. 2021).

Set Realistic Expectations: Manage stakeholder expectations by communicating the AI journey clearly. Highlight quick wins to demonstrate immediate value as well as the long-term potential for optimization (Gans et al. 2018).

Promote Cross-Functional Collaboration: Break down silos between technical teams and business units, creating an environment where diverse perspectives contribute to more robust AI models (Mikalef et al. 2019).

In the end, implementing AI is not solely a technological undertaking but a cultural transformation. Addressing challenges with transparency and fostering trust throughout the organization enables businesses to maximize the potential of AI-enabled pricing strategies.

Ethical Considerations in AI-Enabled Pricing

The integration of AI into pricing strategies opens the door to significant opportunities for businesses, enabling optimized revenue, improved margins, and tailored customer experiences. However, these benefits come with an equally critical obligation to ensure that AI-enabled pricing is implemented ethically, transparently, and fairly. Pricing decisions are more than mathematical outputs; they should reflect a company's values and directly influence customer trust and loyalty (Binns 2018; Martin and Dholakia 2020).

As AI becomes more central to pricing strategies, addressing the ethical dimensions is inevitable not only for compliance but also to protect brand reputation and maintain customer relationships. Areas such as fairness, data privacy, and transparency take center stage in this effort. Ensuring equitable pricing, safeguarding sensitive customer data, and building trust through clear communication are critical for aligning AI-enabled pricing systems with both business goals and societal expectations (Rieke et al. 2020; Gilpin et al. 2018).

This section explores these issues and provides a foundation for understanding how businesses can use AI responsibly to balance profitability with fairness, ensuring the technology serves both organizational objectives and customer interests.

Ensuring Fairness and Avoiding Price Discrimination

Consider this scenario: You are searching online for a flight, and the ticket price unexpectedly rises after revisiting the website a couple of hours later. In frustration, you switch to incognito mode or use a different browser, only to find the original, lower fare reappears. Naturally, you wonder whether the system is profiling you based on your browsing habits.

This exact dilemma caught Monica, a revenue manager at a mid-sized travel platform, after her company introduced an AI-powered dynamic pricing system. The algorithm was designed to adjust ticket prices using real-time demand data, geographic location, and browsing behavior. At first, the system appeared to work well, but customer complaints soon surfaced.

One disgruntled traveler wrote, "My friend and I searched for the same flight sitting side by side, but their ticket was $50 cheaper. Why the difference?" Another accused the company of pricing unfairly based on zip codes, asking, "Are wealthier areas being charged more?"

Monica and her team realized that the AI model, while technically proficient, was unintentionally creating outcomes perceived as unfair by customers. Recognizing the risk to customer trust and brand reputation, they temporarily put the rollout on ice. External ethics consultants were hired to audit the algorithm, leading to the removal of sensitive variables like geographic location and browsing devices that could contribute to discriminatory pricing practices.

The issue of fairness in AI pricing has been a focus of academic research, with Martin and Dholakia (2020) emphasizing the need for pricing algorithms to align with customer expectations to nurture trust. Their work concludes that fairness is not just a technical requirement but a business imperative. Algorithmic decisions should avoid penalizing customers based on uncontrollable factors, such as location or demographic data. Instead, AI-enabled pricing should prioritize equity, ensuring all customers receive a fair experience.

While mathematical optimization can improve profitability, it must be balanced with ethical considerations to cultivate long-term customer loyalty. Companies that place fairness at the center of their AI pricing strategies will not only achieve sustainable growth but also foster trust, strengthening customer relationships in the process (Martin and Dholakia 2020; Rieke et al. 2020).

Data Privacy and Compliance with Regulations

AI-enabled pricing thrives on the use of vast amounts of data to offer insights and personalization. However, with increasing global scrutiny and tighter regulations on data privacy, companies must tread carefully. Mishandling customer information not only risks violating privacy laws but can also undermine consumer trust, a critical factor in sustaining long-term success.

An online fashion retailer learned this lesson the hard way. The German company implemented an AI-powered pricing system that analyzed a combination of customer behavior, purchase history, and social media activity to generate personalized discounts. Initially, the strategy boosted conversion rates and increased revenue. However, a journalist's investigative report revealed that retailer had been sourcing third-party data without clearly informing customers. The backlash was swift, with accusations of invasive practices. Regulators launched an inquiry, citing potential breaches of data privacy laws like the General Data Protection Regulation (GDPR) and the California Consumer Privacy Act (CCPA).

This case highlights a growing tension between innovation and ethical responsibility in AI-enabled pricing. Acquisti et al. (2016) emphasize that companies must prioritize ethical data practices alongside technological advancements, particularly in an era of heightened consumer awareness and stricter privacy regulations.

In response to the controversy, the troubled retailer overhauled its data policies. The company introduced transparency measures, such as giving customers the ability to view and manage the data used to tailor pricing. It also allowed customers to opt out of personalized pricing entirely, partnering with a compliance consultancy to ensure its practices adhered to evolving global standards.

This experience reminds of the importance of proactive transparency and compliance in AI-powered pricing systems. Customers may share their data, but only if they can be assured that it as being handled responsibly and ethically. Companies must strike a careful balance between leveraging data for innovation and safeguarding consumer privacy to foster trust and avoid regulatory pitfalls (Acquisti et al. 2016; Voigt and Von dem Bussche 2017).

Building Trust with Customers Through Transparency

Transparency is fundamental to building trust, particularly when introducing AI-enabled pricing strategies. Customers are more likely to accept and even appreciate dynamic pricing when they understand the logic behind it and perceive it as fair.

Consider the story of a boutique hotel in Spain that adopted an AI-based dynamic pricing system to manage room rates. Initially, guests were confused by frequent price fluctuations, sometimes within hours, which led to complaints and negative reviews accusing the hotel of being inconsistent and overly profit-driven.

Adrian, the hotel manager, decided to adopt a more transparent approach. He added a note next to room prices on the hotel's website, explaining, "Our pricing adjusts in real time to reflect demand, ensuring fair value for all our guests. Booking early guarantees the best rate." This simple message not only clarified the dynamic pricing mechanism but also created a sense of urgency, motivating guests to book earlier.

Adrian also ensured his team was well prepared to address customer concerns. Staff were trained regularly to explain the system's benefits to curious or frustrated guests. For instance, when a last-minute booker complained about higher rates, the receptionist clarified, "It's our policy to ensure that early bookers secure the best deals while minimizing empty rooms. It is transparent and fair to all guests."

This approach resonates with Tene and Polonetsky's (2013) assertion that clear communication about algorithmic decision-making fosters trust and acceptance. Transparency helps demystify AI's role in pricing decisions, ensuring customers feel informed rather than manipulated. Research by Acquisti et al. (2015) further supports this, suggesting that visible and understandable policies regarding technology use improve customer trust and engagement.

The hotel's strategy turned out to fare well. Guests began to appreciate the clarity and fairness of the system, reflected in improved reviews. Some even recommended the hotel because of its honest and straightforward approach, turning initial skepticism into loyalty. This case illustrates that transparency not only mitigates concerns but also enhances customer satisfaction and advocacy.

A Delicate Balance

Ethics in AI-enabled pricing is not about compromising profitability but about balancing between business objectives and customer trust. Companies that embed ethical considerations into their pricing strategies often achieve enhanced long-term outcomes. Ethical pricing practices, anchored in fairness, transparency, and privacy, help build customer loyalty, reduce churn, and bolster brand reputation (Acquisti et al. 2015; Tene and Polonetsky 2013).

The focus must extend beyond immediate financial gains. As seen in the examples discussed earlier, prioritizing fairness and openness in pricing not only mitigates ethical risks but also fosters sustainable growth. When organizations align AI-enabled pricing with their foundational values, they generate enduring value for themselves and their customers (Acquisti et al. 2015).

AI-enabled pricing presents tremendous opportunities. With greater opportunities come also greater responsibilities. Companies must take fairness seriously in pricing decisions, safeguard customer data, and maintain transparency to preserve trust. These actions are not merely ethical imperatives; consider them strategic investments. By implementing AI in a way that aligns with corporate values, organizations can move beyond revenue optimization to build meaningful, lasting customer relationships (Martin and Dholakia 2020).

References

Acquisti A, Brandimarte L, Loewenstein G (2015) Privacy and human behavior in the age of information. Science 347(6221):509–514. https://doi.org/10.1126/science.aaa1465

Acquisti A, Taylor C, Wagman L (2016) The economics of privacy. J Econ Lit 54(2):442–492

Bertsimas D, Kallus N (2020) From predictive to prescriptive analytics. Manag Sci 66(3):1–23. https://doi.org/10.1287/mnsc.2019.3531

Binns A (2018) Responsible AI: a framework for building trust in your AI solutions. Deloitte Insights. Retrieved from https://www2.deloitte.com/content/dam/insights/us/articles/4514_AI-ethics/4514_AIEthics.pdf

Brynjolfsson E, McAfee A (2014) The second machine age: work, progress, and prosperity in a time of brilliant technologies. W.W. Norton & Company

Chen Y, Zhang C, Goh M (2021) Data integration in AI systems: insights from cloud-based platforms. J Bus Intell 34(2):45–59

Choi E, Schuetz A, Safavi M (2021) Data privacy and the future of AI-enabled business intelligence: a study of synthetic data generation. J Bus Anal 9(3):165–179. https://doi.org/10.1016/j.jba.2021.02.005

Choudhury M, Bharadwaj A, Bhatnagar S (2022) Consumer behavior in digital ecosystems: implications for pricing and demand forecasting. J Market Sci 40(1):78–92

Chui M, Manyika J, Miremadi M (2021) The state of AI in 2021. McKinsey & Company. Retrieved from https://www.mckinsey.com

Davenport TH, Ronanki R (2018) Artificial intelligence for the real world. Harv Bus Rev 96(1):108–116

Gans J, Goldfarb A, Agrawal A (2018) Prediction machines: the simple economics of artificial intelligence. Harvard Business Review Press

Gilpin LH, Bau D, Yuan BZ, Melamed T (2018) Explaining explanations: an overview of interpretability of machine learning. Proceedings of the 2018 CHI conference on human factors in computing systems, 1–11. https://doi.org/10.1145/3173574.3173578

Hagel J (2020) The collaboration imperative: unlocking AI's potential in business strategy. Harv Bus Rev 98(2):34–45

Heaton J (2017) Machine learning for business professionals. O'Reilly Media

Kumar A, Shah D (2021) Global pricing strategies: the challenges of customization in diverse markets. J Int Bus Strat 15(3):56–72

Lee S (2019) Adapting AI pricing models to regional market nuances: best practices for global scaling. Int J Pricing Strat 10(4):22–35

Martin KD, Dholakia UM (2020) Algorithmic bias in pricing: perceived fairness and customer trust. J Market Sci 48(3):490–505

McKinsey & Company (2023) How leaders can drive successful AI transformations. Retrieved from https://www.mckinsey.com

Mikalef P, Krogstie J, Pappas IO, Pavlou PA (2019) Agile and lean methodologies in IT governance: an empirical investigation of their application to AI solutions. Inf Manag 56(7):103126. https://doi.org/10.1016/j.im.2019.03.005

Rieke N, Hancox J, Li W, Milletari F, Roth HR, Albarqouni S, Cardoso MJ (2020) The future of federated learning in healthcare AI. Nat Mach Intell 2(6):337–340

Shankar V, Bolton RN (2021) AI and the future of dynamic pricing. J Mark 85(1):34–50

Smith J, Anderson R (2021) Leveraging AI for pricing optimization: a case study of subscription-based pricing models. J Bus Strateg 42(4):60–71

Smith K, Roberts P, Lee M (2022) Real-time AI in retail pricing: challenges and opportunities. Int J Pricing Sci 18(2):112–127

Tene O, Polonetsky J (2013) Big data for all: privacy and user control in the age of analytics. Northwest J Technol Intellect Prop 11(5):239–273

The Alan Turing Institute. (2023). Generative AI for consumer insights and market analysis. Retrieved from https://www.turing.ac.uk

Voigt P, Von dem Bussche A (2017) The EU General Data Protection Regulation (GDPR): a practical guide. Springer International Publishing

5

The Future of AI-Enabled Pricing

Introduction

AI's integration into pricing is not a fleeting trend. It is a pivotal transformation that is reshaping how businesses strategize and compete. Pricing decisions, once reliant on historical data and manual adjustments, are now being powered by systems that can predict, adapt, and evolve in real time. This evolution positions pricing as a strategic lever, influencing customer relationships, profitability, and market positioning (Brynjolfsson and McAfee 2017; Martin and Dholakia 2020).

However, the future of AI in pricing is more profound than technological advancements. It also raises critical questions about the changing roles of pricing professionals and how organizations adapt to these shifts. Will pricing teams engage AI to become key drivers of strategy, or risk being overshadowed by autonomous systems? Furthermore, can AI enhance transparency and fairness in pricing, or will it exacerbate ethical concerns and inequalities (Acquisti et al. 2015; Tene and Polonetsky 2013a)?

This chapter delves into emerging trends shaping AI-enabled pricing, from the development of autonomous pricing systems to the potential integration of blockchain for pricing transparency. Beyond technology, I will explore how pricing professionals can harness these advancements to move beyond operational tasks and position themselves as strategic leaders.

In light of these trends and opportunities, AI in pricing is increasingly emerging as a transformative force that redefines how businesses perceive and deliver value. The challenge is not merely to adopt these innovations but to lead the way in applying them responsibly and effectively.

The future of AI-enabled pricing is unfolding rapidly, offering both promise and challenges. As we navigate this new landscape, pricing professionals have the chance to shape its trajectory, ensuring that AI drives not only profitability but also equity and innovation in an ever-evolving business environment.

Trends Shaping the Future

The evolution of AI in pricing is unmistakably accelerating, transitioning from being a novel competitive advantage to a foundational capability that businesses cannot afford to overlook. The future of pricing strategies will be characterized by profound technological advancements and broader changes in how companies approach value creation. Emerging trends highlight a shift toward pricing systems that are not only dynamic and data-driven but also adaptive, interconnected, and aligned with rapidly changing customer expectations (Brynjolfsson and McAfee 2017; Martin and Dholakia 2020).

These trends corroborate a move toward real-time pricing models enabled by advanced machine learning algorithms, increased integration with broader digital ecosystems, and the adoption of customer-centric approaches that ensure both personalization and fairness. As companies continue to brace for these innovations, pricing will play a pivotal role in shaping competitive landscapes and driving sustainable business growth (Tene and Polonetsky 2013b; Chui et al. 2021).

Autonomous Systems and AI Agents: Leveling Up Decision-Making in Real Time

Autonomous systems, driven by advanced reinforcement learning, machine learning, and real-time data analysis, are fundamentally transforming pricing strategies. These systems dynamically adjust prices by continuously analyzing variables such as demand fluctuations, competitive activities, and external market conditions. Their adaptive nature allows businesses to implement data-driven decision-making at unprecedented speed and scale (Brynjolfsson and McAfee 2017).

At the heart of these autonomous systems are AI agents, i.e., sophisticated decision-makers that operate with minimal human intervention. Unlike traditional pricing tools, which are heavily dependent on static rules or manual adjustments, AI agents are able to leverage reinforcement learning to interact with their environments and improve outcomes over time. This capability enables continuous optimization of pricing strategies, capturing fleeting market opportunities, and mitigating risks effectively.

Large e-commerce platforms engage AI agents to analyze thousands of SKUs, incorporating variables such as consumer purchasing behavior, competitor pricing, and seasonal trends to recommend or implement optimal prices. Such systems have demonstrated significant improvements in efficiency and revenue generation by reducing reliance on manual pricing processes (Talluri and van Ryzin 2004). Similarly, in the ride-hailing industry, AI agents dynamically adjust fares based on real-time demand surges, balancing profitability with driver and customer satisfaction.

Recent advancements have further enhanced these systems. Modern AI agents integrate multimodal data sources, such as geospatial analytics and even customer sentiment mined from social media, enabling a richer understanding of market dynamics. They employ explainable AI (XAI) techniques to make their decision-making processes transparent, fostering trust among stakeholders (Gunning and Aha 2019).

In spite of their capabilities, AI agents raise concerns pertaining to transparency and fairness. Customers may perceive price changes as arbitrary or exploitative if the reasoning behind such adjustments is opaque. To mitigate these concerns, businesses are adopting strategies to enhance transparency. Visual tools and explanatory mechanisms, such as showing how demand-supply dynamics influence pricing, have proven effective in building consumer trust. For example, ride-hailing platforms often display pricing breakdowns or fare calculators, helping customers make sense of price variations (Wirtz et al. 2022a, b). Furthermore, ethical considerations are gaining prominence, with companies prioritizing fairness and inclusivity in their AI-driven pricing strategies (Floridi et al. 2018).

AI agents are expected to grow more sophisticated in the coming years. Emerging technologies, such as synthetic data generation and federated learning, are equipping these systems with the ability to learn from diverse, decentralized datasets without compromising privacy. Additionally, developments in edge computing are enabling real-time pricing decisions closer to the point of transaction, reducing latency and improving responsiveness.

Moreover, AI agents are increasingly being tailored to organizational values and customer expectations. This involves embedding ethical principles into their design and operation, ensuring that pricing strategies remain fair and non-discriminatory (Chui et al. 2021). Businesses that successfully balance efficiency, transparency, and fairness will be best positioned to harness the full potential of autonomous pricing systems.

Green AI: Integrating Sustainability and Pricing

Green AI is rapidly becoming a key element in the development of modern pricing strategies, especially as businesses face mounting pressure to reduce their environmental impact. This approach is not solely centered on boosting profits; it emphasizes the integration of sustainability into core business practices, with AI playing a crucial role in making pricing decisions that promote eco-friendly practices. By leveraging AI, businesses are enhancing supply chain operations, improving energy efficiency, and reducing waste, all of which contribute to more sustainable practices (Cohen et al. 2021).

For example, a European grocery retailer implemented AI-enabled solutions to adjust discounts on perishable items nearing expiration. This adjustment led to a 30% reduction in food waste, while also improving profit margins by 10% (European Commission 2023). These AI-based pricing models not only minimized the amount of unsold inventory but also ensured the pricing reflected the actual value of goods nearing their shelf life. This is a clear example of how Green AI can effectively combine sustainability with profitability, allowing businesses to reduce waste and optimize resource use in real time (PwC 2023).

The growing trend of Green AI also mirrors a shift in consumer preferences. A recent study by PwC (2023) revealed that 57% of consumers prioritize eco-friendly products, indicating that sustainability is becoming a key consideration in consumer purchasing decisions. For businesses, this trend presents an opportunity to create stronger bonds with customers by incorporating sustainability into pricing strategies, enhancing customer loyalty (Chui et al. 2021).

The adoption of Green AI also contributes to global sustainability initiatives. Experts like Cohen et al. (2021) highlight how AI can optimize resource consumption and reduce energy use in sectors such as manufacturing and retail. For instance, AI systems are increasingly being deployed to adjust energy prices dynamically, based on real-time demand and grid conditions, facilitating more sustainable energy distribution (Cohen et al. 2021). As AI technology advances, its role in sustainable pricing strategies will only expand, offering businesses the chance to improve both their bottom lines and their environmental impact.

Consequently, businesses must balance technological advancements with the broader societal expectations for sustainability. The future of pricing will not only involve determining the right price for products, but also considering the environmental impact of those products and ensuring sustainability is central to pricing strategies (Brynjolfsson and McAfee 2017).

Ecosystem Pricing: The Dynamic Marketplace

Ecosystem pricing, where pricing decisions are shaped by interconnected systems across various sectors, is increasingly being recognized as a powerful model. In smart cities, for example, AI-powered systems can be trusted with managing everything from parking to waste disposal to air quality, adjusting prices in real time based on factors such as local events or traffic conditions. This interconnected approach not only improves operational efficiency but also enhances customer experiences by aligning pricing with current demand and environmental factors.

In the energy sector, dynamic pricing has also made significant strides. Smart meters, coupled with AI algorithms, allow utilities to adjust electricity prices based on fluctuations in demand or changes in weather conditions. This pricing model benefits consumers by offering lower rates during off-peak hours while optimizing energy distribution (Smart Energy International 2023). Similarly, industries like ride-hailing and airlines are using AI to adjust their prices based on external variables such as weather patterns, balancing revenue maximization with competitive pricing strategies.

These developments exemplify a transition from static pricing models to interconnected, real-time systems, in which multiple external influences guide pricing decisions. Ecosystem pricing illustrates the potential of AI to create flexible and adaptive pricing strategies that deliver value to both consumers and businesses, while fostering efficiency and responsiveness in the marketplace.

Security and Ethical Considerations in AI-Enabled Pricing

As AI systems manage sensitive customer and transaction data, ensuring robust security has become a top priority. More and more companies have begun to employ cybersecurity tools to safeguard their pricing platforms from potential breaches. For instance, a logistics company utilized anomaly detection algorithms to monitor and protect its freight pricing system, allowing it to flag unusual activities and prevent unauthorized access (ShipScience 2023).

In addition to security, ethical considerations remain at the forefront of AI-enabled pricing strategies. Transparent, fair, and unbiased pricing not only ensures compliance but also cultivates trust and fosters long-term customer loyalty. Tene and Polonetsky (2013a) claim that companies that focus on fairness and explainability in their AI models mitigate reputational risks and set themselves up for sustainable growth.

A Look Ahead

The trends currently shaping AI in pricing are transforming how businesses perceive value, customer relationships, and transparency. Emerging technologies like autonomous systems and blockchain are improving efficiency and building trust, while advances in AI models are enabling companies to achieve unprecedented levels of precision and creativity in their pricing strategies. Moreover, the development of ecosystem pricing is fostering greater collaboration across industries, breaking down traditional silos and driving more dynamic and responsive pricing practices.

As these innovations keep unfolding, they are not only shaping the future of pricing but also redefining what it means for businesses to lead in a rapidly evolving landscape.

A Vision for Pricing Professionals

As artificial intelligence increasingly shapes the field of pricing, it is not only revving up the processes behind pricing decisions but also redefining the roles of those who drive them. Pricing professionals should evolve from being mere custodians of numbers to becoming strategic architects, innovators, and communicators of value. This role change offers an opportunity for pricing teams to assume a more prominent and influential position within their organizations. By embracing these changes, they can lead the charge in driving smarter, data-informed decisions that effectively enhance business performance and customer satisfaction (Brynjolfsson and McAfee 2017; Chui et al. 2020). As AI continues to advance, pricing professionals will find themselves in positions that require not only analytical skills but also the ability to drive strategic growth and foster a culture of continuous innovation.

How AI Transforms the Role of Pricing Teams

In the past, pricing teams often worked in isolation, confining themselves to spreadsheets and cost sheets to adjust prices based on past performance. They typically reacted to market shifts after they had already occurred, with little foresight or strategic input. However, the integration of artificial intelligence has fundamentally changed this reactive approach, elevating pricing into a proactive and dynamic function.

A notable example of this shift occurred at a global automotive supplier, where the pricing team moved from a historical analysis model to one focused on forecasting future opportunities. With the help of AI-enabled models, the team could now predict how price adjustments would affect customer behavior months in advance. This allowed them to move beyond the question of "What price worked last year?" to instead consider, "What price will drive growth in the upcoming year?"

Such a transformation requires new competencies. Pricing professionals must not only be able to interpret AI-generated insights but also communicate them effectively across the organization. Additionally, aligning pricing strategies with broader business goals is essential. As Hinterhuber and Liozu (2013) emphasize, pricing leaders need to evolve into "value architects," blending technical expertise with strategic vision to drive business success (Kumar and Shah 2021).

The Shift from Tactical Pricing to Strategic Leadership

One of the most exciting developments in AI-enabled pricing is how it empowers pricing professionals to assume strategic leadership roles. By automating routine tasks such as data analysis and price adjustments, AI empowers teams to shift their focus to higher-level, more strategic concerns, such as:

- How can we ensure that our pricing strategy aligns with the company's long-term objectives?
- What new market opportunities can predictive insights help us uncover?
- How can pricing become a tool for fostering customer loyalty and enhancing brand differentiation?

A case in point is a SaaS company that made use of AI to improve its subscription pricing strategy. Before implementing AI, the pricing team was bogged down by managing promotional discounts and responding to escalations from the sales team. After introducing AI, the team had more capacity to collaborate with marketing and product teams. Together, they developed a value-based pricing strategy, tailoring subscription packages to various customer segments. This collaborative effort resulted in a 20% increase in average revenue per user.

This trend highlights the growing role of pricing professionals as key contributors to strategic decisions. As Phillips (2005) notes, pricing is no longer about crunching numbers; it is more about creating and communicating value. By integrating pricing strategies with other departments, pricing professionals are transforming into vital players who influence a company's competitive edge and long-term success.

AI as an Enabler, Not a Substitute

Although AI offers powerful capabilities, it is essential to recognize that it is not meant to supersede human judgment but rather to augment it. The most effective pricing decisions continue to rely on factors such as context, creativity, and empathy, qualities that AI cannot replicate yet.

For example, an e-commerce company utilized AI to examine customer purchasing behaviors and recommended price increases for popular products. While the data supported these suggestions, the pricing team realized that the timing of the price hikes coincided with a major public holiday. They were concerned that raising prices during a festive period could be perceived as profiteering. Instead, the team chose to implement more modest price adjustments, complete with value-added promotions, such as bundled offers and loyalty rewards, to maintain customer goodwill.

As Bertsimas and Kallus (2020) argue, while prescriptive analytics can provide valuable guidance, the final decision should always consider the subtleties of human behavior and cultural contexts. In other words, AI should support, not replace, human decision-making.

The Opportunity Ahead

The emergence of AI does not reduce the importance of pricing professionals. On the contrary, it enhances it. As AI evolves, it provides pricing teams with the tools to lead strategically, leverage data-driven insights, and advocate for fair pricing practices. This shift presents a unique opportunity for today's pricing experts to shape the future of commerce by using AI to drive smarter, more informed decisions.

To succeed in this AI-enabled landscape, pricing professionals must be:

1. **Strategic Thinkers:** Capable of aligning pricing decisions with broader business goals and anticipating market shifts.
2. **Data Storytellers:** Proficient in translating complex AI insights into clear, actionable narratives that resonate with stakeholders.
3. **Ethical Stewards:** Dedicated to maintaining fairness, transparency, and ethical considerations in all pricing practices.

While this transformation may take time to unfold, the rewards are substantial. Pricing professionals who embrace this evolving role will not only elevate their careers but also contribute to their organizations' success in an increasingly AI-powered world (Chui et al. 2021; Tene and Polonetsky 2013a).

A Glimpse into Tomorrow's Pricing Teams

Imagine a scenario in 2035 where pricing teams are the driving force behind innovation within organizations. These teams collaborate closely with data scientists to experiment with state-of-the-art pricing models, work hand-in-hand with marketing to develop personalized offers, and provide crucial insights to executives on how to adapt to global changes and disruptions.

Rather than being overshadowed by AI, these pricing professionals are at the forefront of change, utilizing technology to enhance decision-making in ways that are faster, smarter, and more ethically grounded. No longer confined to the back office, they are now seen as key drivers of growth, shaping how businesses connect with customers and create value in the marketplace.

This vision of the future is not just a dream; it is a tangible reality that can be realized through the decisions pricing professionals make today. As AI continues to evolve, embracing these changes will empower teams to take on increasingly strategic roles, leading organizations toward greater success (Brynjolfsson and McAfee 2017; Chui et al. 2021).

Departing Thoughts

As we conclude this exploration of AI-enabled pricing, it is worth reflecting on the remarkable progress we have made and where we are headed. Pricing has long been a delicate balance of analysis and intuition, but AI is significantly tipping the scale, providing unparalleled precision, flexibility, and growth opportunities.

As a horizontal enabling layer, AI is set to change the way how pricing works across all organizations. Ignoring AI is not really a viable option. Just like Jensen Huang aptly put, "AI is not going to take your job. The person who uses AI will" (Huang 2023). Analogically, a company that does not use AI in pricing will lose its competitive edge to a competitor that does.

Throughout this book, we have examined how AI is transforming pricing strategies, from predicting customer behavior with impressive accuracy to enabling dynamic, real-time price adjustments. AI is revolutionizing pricing and creating new opportunities.

However, with these opportunities come responsibilities, ones that require thoughtful leadership, a clear strategic vision, and a dedication to ethical standards. The future of pricing is not just about algorithms; it is about how business leaders leverage these tools to drive organizational success. AI thrives in an environment where human creativity and judgment are married with technology.

Adopting AI for pricing is a continuous process. This shift demands a cultural change, where teams are open to modern technology, trust data, and view AI as a collaborator. The most successful AI implementations prioritize education, transparency, and engagement, ensuring that teams feel confident and empowered. As AI continues to evolve, leaders will need to strike a balance between innovation, ethics, profitability, and fairness. These principles will guide AI-enabled pricing strategies that foster customer trust and long-term business success.

Imagine yourself in 2035, leading a team that drives innovation and creates value for the business, customers, and partners. The decisions you make today will lay the foundation for that success. The future of AI-enabled pricing is bright, but it requires leaders like you to take the first step.

So, as you wrap up and reflect on this book, ask yourselves:

- *What will be the next pricing challenge you tackle with AI?*
- *How will you make an impact in your organization or industry?*
- *What unique value can you unlock by leveraging AI in pricing that wasn't possible before?*
- *How will you align AI-enabled pricing strategies with your organization's long-term vision and values?*
- *What steps will you take to ensure your pricing solutions remain ethical, customer-focused, and adaptable in an ever-changing market?*
- *How can you use AI to elevate pricing from a tactical function to a key driver of sustainable growth and innovation?*

- *What partnerships, skills, or resources will you prioritize to fully realize the potential of AI in pricing?*
- …

These questions are an invitation to think beyond the practical applications and explore the transformative power of AI-enabled pricing. The journey is just beginning. Be part of it.

References

Acquisti A, Brandimarte L, Loewenstein G (2015) Privacy and human behavior in the age of information. Science 347(6221):509–514. https://doi.org/10.1126/science.aaa1465

Bertsimas D, Kallus N (2020) From predictive to prescriptive analytics: achieving business optimization with AI. Manag Sci 66(3):1–23. https://doi.org/10.1287/mnsc.2019.3531

Brynjolfsson E, McAfee A (2017) The second machine age: work, progress, and prosperity in a time of brilliant technologies. W.W. Norton & Company

Chui M, Manyika J, Miremadi M (2020) The next normal in AI adoption: the road to a responsible and efficient future. McKinsey & Company. https://www.mckinsey.com/featured-insights/artificial-intelligence/the-next-normal-in-ai-adoption

Chui M, Manyika J, Miremadi M (2021). The state of AI in 2021. McKinsey & Company. https://www.mckinsey.com/featured-insights/artificial-intelligence/the-state-of-ai-in-2021

Cohen S, Ross J, Iansiti M (2021) How AI can drive sustainability in business. Harvard Business Review. https://hbr.org

European Food Retail AI Integration Committee (2023) European food retail AI integration report.

Floridi L, Cowls J, King T, Taddeo M (2018) AI for social good: ethics and transparency in AI. Sci Eng Ethics 24(5):412–432

Gunning D, Aha D (2019) Explainable artificial intelligence (XAI): concepts, taxonomies, opportunities. AI Mag 40(2):34–46

Hinterhuber A, Liozu SM (2013) Innovation in pricing: contemporary theories and best practices. Routledge

Huang J (2023, March 21) AI: the future of computing with NVIDIA CEO Jensen Huang [Video]. YouTube. https://www.youtube.com/watch?v=SwIYoUk1Y_s

Kumar A, Shah D (2021) Global pricing strategies: the challenges of customization in diverse markets. J Int Bus Strat 15(3):56–72

Martin KD, Dholakia UM (2020) Fostering customer trust through ethical AI practices. J Bus Ethics 163(4):705–718. https://doi.org/10.1007/s10551-019-04360-4

Phillips R (2005) Pricing and revenue optimization. Stanford University Press

PwC (2023) Consumer intelligence series: how sustainability drives consumer preferences. PricewaterhouseCoopers

ShipScience (2023, October 26) 7 use cases showing the benefits of anomaly detection in the logistics industry through machine learning. ShipScience. Retrieved from https://www.shipscience.com/7-use-cases-showing-the-benefits-of-anomaly-detection-in-the-logistics-industry-through-machine-learning-9c1ef/

Smart Energy International (2023, November 15) 128 million smart meters in US in 2023. Smart Energy International. Retrieved from https://www.smart-energy.com/regional-news/north-america/128-million-smart-meters-in-us-in-2023/

Talluri KT, van Ryzin GJ (2004) The theory and practice of revenue management. Springer

Tene O, Polonetsky J (2013a) Big data for all: privacy and user control in the age of analytics. Northwest J Technol Intellect Prop 11(5):239–273

Tene O, Polonetsky J (2013b) Privacy in the age of big data: a time for big decisions. Stanford Law Rev 66(4):37–53. https://doi.org/10.2139/ssrn.2361972

Wirtz J, So KKF, Mody MA, Liu SQ, Chun HH (2022a) Platforms in the sharing economy: understanding the dynamic relationship between platforms and their users. J Mark 86(1):48–69

Wirtz J, Zeithaml VA, Kimes SE (2022b) Services marketing: People, technology, strategy. Pearson

Appendix: Mastering AI Prompts for Smarter Pricing Advice

Introduction

If there is one thing that I have learned from co-piloting with ChatGPT or any other AI chatbot, it is that asking the right question is half the battle. Early on, I found myself frustrated when responses missed the mark until it hit me: the problem was not the tool; it was me. I was not being clear, specific, or deliberate enough in my prompts. Once I started thinking more carefully about how I was asking, everything changed. The insights became sharper, the suggestions more relevant, and the conversations genuinely helpful.

This realization felt personal but also oddly universal, especially for pricing professionals like us. In pricing, precision is everything. We live in a world where one overlooked assumption or poorly framed scenario can lead to a domino effect of bad decisions. It is no different with AI. Generative AI Tools like ChatGPT can serve personal efficiency boosters, helping us analyze markets, simulate scenarios, or generate recommendations, but they are only as good as the instructions we feed them.

This bonus chapter is my attempt to share what I have learned, both through trial and error and plenty of playful back-and-forth with ChatGPT and Co. I would like to offer practical tips that can help you harness AI in a way that feels empowering instead of frustrating. Whether you are an analyst, a consultant, or an executive, I think you will find them as useful as I have.

Why Prompt Optimization Matters in Pricing

Being an intricate discipline, pricing requires in-depth knowledge of markets, competitors, customers, and internal financial goals. The stakes are high: The wrong pricing strategy can erode revenue, damage customer trust, or create operational inefficiencies. AI tools like ChatGPT and Gemini can assist by:

- **Generating market insights:** Summarizing trends, competitor pricing data, and consumer behaviors.
- **Simulating pricing scenarios:** Modeling potential outcomes for price adjustments or promotional offers.
- **Developing pricing strategies:** Recommending approaches such as dynamic pricing, bundling, or segmentation-specific pricing.

However, an AI chatbot is not inherently "intelligent." The quality of its responses depends to a large extent on how well a user frames the question. Poorly constructed prompts can lead to irrelevant, vague, or misleading outputs. Mastering prompt design helps bridge this gap, unleashing the full potential of AI as a powerful assistant that complements pricing expertise.

Key Principles of Effective Prompt Design for Pricing

1. **Be Specific and Clear**
   Clear and specific prompts prevent misinterpretation and ensure the AI delivers outputs relevant to your goals. This principle is especially important in pricing, where nuances can make or break a strategy.
   Example:
   - **Weak Prompt:** "What's a good pricing strategy?"
   - **Optimized Prompt:** "What pricing strategies would you recommend for a direct-to-consumer local skincare brand aiming to increase customer acquisition while maintaining a 20% profit margin?"

The optimized version specifies the industry, business goals, and a key financial constraint, providing clarity for a targeted response.

Appendix: Mastering AI Prompts for Smarter Pricing Advice

2. **Set the Context**
   Context shapes how AI interprets your prompt. Pricing decisions depend on factors like industry dynamics, target customer segments, and regional variations. Including these details in your prompt improves relevance.
   Example:
   - **Contextualized Prompt:** "I'm conducting a pricing analysis for an e-commerce brand selling premium coffee products in the North American market. What factors should I consider to optimize pricing for subscription plans to increase market share and revenue?"

This example provides the product category, market, and pricing model, ensuring that the AI chatbot delivers advice tailored to these specifics.

3. **Break Down Complex Questions**
   Pricing involves multiple layers, such as value assessment, cost analysis, elasticity estimation, and competitor benchmarking. Rather than asking one broad question, breaking it into smaller, concise prompts allows the AI chatbot to address each aspect more thoroughly.
   Example:
   - Part 1: "What are the main advantages and disadvantages of cost-plus pricing for a small manufacturing business?"
   - Part 2: "How can a manufacturing business incorporate competitor pricing into a value-based pricing strategy?"
   - Part 3 (less obvious, but powerful): "What else should I ask you to define the best pricing strategy for my manufacturing business?"

Segmenting questions like this ensures that no critical details are overlooked.

Toolbox: Advanced Techniques for Prompt Optimization

1. **Use Role Assignments to Refine Perspective**
   Assigning a role to the AI chatbot, such as "pricing manager" or "chief growth officer," shapes the tone and approach of its response.
   Example:
   - **Role-Based Prompt:** "As a pricing manager for a mid-sized retail chain, how would you approach setting seasonal discounts for high-margin products?"

This role helps the AI chatbot respond as though it were in a professional pricing position, delivering more focused and contextually relevant advice.

2. **Leverage Scenario Simulations**

   AI chatbots excel at generating hypothetical scenarios that mirror real-world pricing challenges. Including scenarios in your prompts enables the AI to model potential outcomes.

   Example:
   - **Scenario-Based Prompt:** "A SaaS company is considering a price increase for its basic subscription plan. Simulate potential customer reactions and recommend strategies to minimize churn."

By providing a specific situation, this prompt ensures actionable insights.

3. **Request Step-by-Step Processes**

   Pricing strategies often require multi-step processes, from data collection to decision-making. Asking for a step-by-step explanation encourages clarity and depth.

   Example:
   - **Step-by-Step Prompt:** "Explain the steps to calculate customer lifetime value (CLV) and how it can inform pricing decisions for a subscription-based business."

This approach provides structured guidance that can be easily followed or adapted.

4. **Incorporate Constraints**

   Constraints, such as word limits or specific formats, guide the AI chatbot produce more concise and relevant outputs.

   Example:
   - **With Constraints:** "Summarize the pros and cons of dynamic pricing for e-commerce in under 200 words, focusing on customer trust and operational challenges."

Constraints help refine the response, making it easier to apply in professional settings.

5. **Encourage Multi-Perspective Analysis**

   Pricing decisions benefit from considering diverse perspectives. Prompting the AI chatbot to explore various viewpoints enriches the response.

Example:
- **Prompt:** "Analyze the pros and cons of freemium pricing from the perspectives of a startup founder, an end-user, a competitor, and an investor."

This ensures a balanced analysis that factors in different stakeholders' needs and expectations.

Application Examples

1. **Dynamic Pricing in E-Commerce**
   Dynamic pricing, where prices fluctuate based on demand, competitor behavior, or inventory levels, is a common AI-enabled approach.
   Prompt Example:
   - "How can an online retailer use AI to implement dynamic pricing while maintaining customer trust and avoiding price discrimination backlash?"

   AI chatbots can suggest actionable strategies like transparent pricing policies or customer segmentation, making this prompt highly practical.

2. **Price Elasticity Analysis**
   Understanding how sensitive customers are to price changes is critical for pricing optimization.
   Prompt Example:
   - "Provide step-by-step guidance on how to calculate price elasticity for a retail clothing brand and explain how to use this data to set optimal markdown levels during sales."

   This ensures the output is directly applicable to pricing teams looking for precision in markdown strategies.

3. **Bundling and Cross-Selling Strategies**
   Bundling can enhance perceived value and increase average transaction size.
   Prompt Example:
   - "What are the best practices for designing bundle pricing for a subscription service offering fitness classes and nutritional plans?"

   AI chatbots can generate strategies for maximizing revenue while maintaining simplicity and customer satisfaction.

Overcoming Limitations and Iterative Refinement

Even with optimized prompts, AI chatbots may not always deliver perfect results. Iterative refinement can address this:

1. **Identify Gaps:**
   If the response feels incomplete, ask follow-up questions.
   Example: "Could you provide more detail on how competitor analysis influences value-based pricing?"
2. **Rephrase Prompts:**
   Misinterpreted prompts can be rephrased for clarity.
   Example: Original: "What's a good pricing strategy?"
   Revised: "How can a premium beverage brand use penetration pricing to gain market share in a new region?"
3. **Combine Outputs:**
   For complex questions, combine responses from multiple prompts.
   Example: Use separate prompts for cost analysis, customer segmentation, and competitive benchmarking, then synthesize the results.
4. **Play Devil's Advocate:**
   Challenge the strength of the response. Make the chatbot debate with itself.
   Example: "How confident are you in the pricing recommendation that you just provided?"

Practical Integration of AI Chatbots into Pricing Workflows

To conclude, let's go over how pricing professionals can effectively use AI chatbots to enhance their work:

1. **Automating Routine Tasks:** Use the AI chatbot for generating quick summaries of competitor pricing trends or customer feedback.
2. **Brainstorming Ideas:** Explore innovative pricing strategies with open-ended prompts like "Suggest creative discount structures for a new product launch."
3. **Training and Collaboration:** Use the AI chatbot as a training tool for junior team members, helping them grasp complex pricing concepts.

The Power of Optimized Prompts

By consciously designing your prompts, you will be surprised by what AI chatbots have to offer. Whether you are generating insights, simulating scenarios, or refining strategies, prompt design is the key to achieving high-quality outputs. Through precise, iterative, and creative prompt crafting, you can make the better of it.

One More Thing

Stay hungry, stay young, stay foolish, stay curious, and stay vigilant because just when you think you got all the answers is the moment when some bitter twist of fate in the universe will remind you that you very much don't.

GPSR Compliance

The European Union's (EU) General Product Safety Regulation (GPSR) is a set of rules that requires consumer products to be safe and our obligations to ensure this.

If you have any concerns about our products, you can contact us on

ProductSafety@springernature.com

In case Publisher is established outside the EU, the EU authorized representative is:

Springer Nature Customer Service Center GmbH
Europaplatz 3
69115 Heidelberg, Germany

www.ingramcontent.com/pod-product-compliance
Lightning Source LLC
LaVergne TN
LVHW010342260326
834688LV00036B/843